"We have social media friendships, idolizing friendships, self-seeking friendships and other friend-ish relationships. Kelly Needham skillfully points us toward true biblical friendships. She shows us the beauty and necessity of biblical friendships and the ways friendships can assume the wrong place. With good-hearted and wise counsel, Kelly helps us see friendship as God intends it to be."

—RANDY ALCORN, AUTHOR OF *HEAVEN*, *HAPPINESS*, AND *SAFELY HOME*

"How blessed I am to call Kelly Needham 'friend.' And how grateful I am that she has written this important and timely book. Kelly helps us identify ways we may be missing out on the gift of true friendship by settling for counterfeits. And she points us to Christ, the sweetest Friend of all, who alone can fill the deepest longings of our hearts and whose presence enriches and enlivens our human friendships."

—NANCY DEMOSS WOLGEMUTH, AUTHOR AND FOUNDER
AND HOST OF REVIVE OUR HEARTS

"Calling everyone who has or longs for a BFF—are the relationships growing in your friendship-garden weeds or flowers? *Friend-ish* can help you tell the difference. This insightful and engaging book will challenge you to develop deep, authentic, kingdom-building friendships. The kind that will only flourish as you learn to first be best friends with God."

—MARY A. KASSIAN, AUTHOR OF *GIRLS GONE
WISE* AND *THE RIGHT KIND OF STRONG*

"It's rare for a book to model its subject, but *Friend-ish* actually demonstrates real friendship. It is relational and honest and enjoyable. It is willing to diagnose and press on the difficult aspects of life, relationships, and sin. It convicts and encourages, and not in a trite or fluffy way. Most importantly, it draws on Scripture and points to Jesus uncompromisingly and clearly throughout. Kelly also offers keen, incisive observations about cultural trends and personal experiences in friendship. *Friend-ish* is smart, discerning, and godly—a profoundly helpful book for men and women seeking better friendships and to be better friends."

—BARNABAS PIPER, AUTHOR AND PODCASTER

"Friendship is a gift of grace from God, yet inexplicably we as Christians often take our cues regarding friendship from the culture. We simply don't know what it means to enjoy friendship in the way God intended. Thankfully, in *Friend-ish*, Kelly Needham gives us a thoroughly biblical and deeply practical resource, calling us to resist unhealthy friendships and find the better joy in those that stir our affections for Christ."

—CHRISTINE HOOVER, AUTHOR OF *MESSY BEAUTIFUL FRIENDSHIP* AND *WITH ALL YOUR HEART: LIVING JOYFULLY THROUGH ALLEGIANCE TO KING JESUS*

"Every culture in the world has its own counterfeit version of friendship. All of us need the real thing—friendship the way God intended it—but how do we know if what we've got is the real thing? In *Friend-ish*, Needham helps us examine a high definition picture of friendships in American culture, and the floodlight of Scripture shines on every page. This book will help you see things about friendship that you've not seen before through the lens of a Scripture-saturated perspective.

—GLORIA FURMAN, AUTHOR OF *LABOR WITH HOPE* AND *JOYFULLY SPREADING THE WORD*

"I can't think of a better person to speak to the value of healthy friendships than Kelly Needham! Kelly and Jimmy Needham have been dear friends to Donna and I for decades. Kelly has a deep reverence for the word of God and a genuine concern for people. I have watched them leave a wake of blessing behind them as they have loved young men and women well. I am excited to see how this resource helps friendships flourish!"

—BEN STUART, PASTOR OF PASSION CITY CHURCH IN WASHINGTON DC AND AUTHOR OF *SINGLE, DATING, ENGAGED, MARRIED*

"Kelly Needham encourages us to have a view of friendship that is gospel-centered and rooted in our friendship with God. She urges and equips us to embrace friendships that are joyful and meaningful, while reminding us to find our identity and worth in Christ alone."

—KRISTIN SCHMUCKER, FOUNDER OF THE DAILY GRACE CO.

"Grace-driven and refreshingly honest, Kelly Needham has contributed a thoughtful and practical vision for healthy friendships. She graciously challenges our idolatrous tendencies in this arena and opens us up to the joy, freedom, and kingdom potential of Christ-centered relationships."

—JR VASSAR, LEAD PASTOR OF CHURCH AT THE CROSS AND AUTHOR OF
GLORY HUNGER: GOD, THE GOSPEL, AND OUR QUEST FOR SOMETHING MORE

"Friendships are so weird and beautiful and awkward and glorious all at the same time. The older I've gotten, the more I've understood the utter necessity of them but sin, as it always does, can make our friendships more dysfunctional than fruitful. God is calling us into the kind of friendship that will make us better (or should I say holier) leading us to glorify God as best we can. I'm thankful that Kelly Needham's book *Friend-ish* can assist us in that pursuit. I wish I had this book ages ago. Maybe I would've been a better friend and had healthier friendships but then again, I'm still learning both and I always will be. For that reason, I think it would be safe to say that Kelly has been a good friend to us all by writing a book that will help us learn how to do the same."

—JACKIE HILL-PERRY, SPEAKER, POET, ARTIST, AND AUTHOR OF *GAY GIRL,
GOOD GOD: THE STORY OF WHO I WAS, AND WHO GOD HAS ALWAYS BEEN*

"This book is solid and bold. It was difficult to put down because it scratched an itch in my heart to better understand authentic friendship so we can experience it. It made me want to be a comrade-friend with Kelly."

—DANNAH GRESH, BESTSELLING AUTHOR AND FOUNDER OF TRUE GIRL

"*Friend-ish* equips the saints to foster friendships as an act of true worship. Kelly Needham's book will help God's people foster God-centered friendships."

—DAVID NASSER, AUTHOR, PASTOR, AND SENIOR
VICE PRESIDENT AT LIBERTY UNIVERSITY

"The friends we make and keep will define our lives in ways none of us fully appreciate now. I can summarize the story of my life, chapter by chapter, with my friendships. I am the man I am because of the friends God has given me. So, I love the big, God-soaked vision of friendship Kelly Needham paints in *Friend-ish*. The joy of good friendship is a shared joy in God, and our only guide to good friendship is the only book we have from God. Kelly overflows with that joy, and anchors herself in that Book. Friendship is precious and indispensable, yet can be dangerous. This book will help you find the friends you need and be that friend for others."

—MARSHALL SEGAL, MANAGING EDITOR AT
DESIRINGGOD.ORG AND AUTHOR OF *NOT YET MARRIED*

"I look back over my past seasons of life—high school, college, my twenties, and my thirties—and I see the challenges of navigating friendships in those seasons. I think of how words like these would have brought deep clarity and perspective. Kelly's book is more than a handbook for friendship; it's a lighthouse, offering the light of his perspective through his Word to the deep and potentially murky waters of our friendships."

—SARA HAGERTY, BESTSELLING AUTHOR OF *UNSEEN:
THE GIFT OF BEING HIDDEN IN A WORLD THAT LOVES TO
BE NOTICED* AND *EVERY BITTER THING IS SWEET*

friendish

friend*ish*

RECLAIMING REAL FRIENDSHIP IN

A CULTURE OF CONFUSION

KELLY NEEDHAM

NELSON
BOOKS

An Imprint of Thomas Nelson

Published in Nashville, Tennessee, by Nelson Books, an imprint of Thomas Nelson. Nelson Books and Thomas Nelson are registered trademarks of HarperCollins Christian Publishing, Inc.

Published in association with literary agency Wolgemuth & Associates, Inc.

Thomas Nelson titles may be purchased in bulk for educational, business, fund-raising, or sales promotional use. For information, please e-mail SpecialMarkets@ThomasNelson.com.

All names and some identifying details have been changed to protect the privacy of individuals.

Unless otherwise noted, Scripture quotations are taken from the ESV® Bible (The Holy Bible, English Standard Version®). Copyright © 2001 by Crossway, a publishing ministry of Good News Publishers. Used by permission. All rights reserved.

Scripture quotations marked NASB are from New American Standard Bible®. Copyright © 1960, 1962, 1963, 1968, 1971, 1972, 1973, 1975, 1977, 1995 by The Lockman Foundation. Used by permission. (www.Lockman.org)

Scripture quotations marked CSB have been taken from the Christian Standard Bible®, Copyright © 2017 by Holman Bible Publishers. Used by permission. Christian Standard Bible® and CSB® are federally registered trademarks of Holman Bible Publishers.

All emphases in Scripture quotations are the author's.

Any Internet addresses, phone numbers, or company or product information printed in this book are offered as a resource and are not intended in any way to be or to imply an endorsement by Thomas Nelson, nor does Thomas Nelson vouch for the existence, content, or services of these sites, phone numbers, companies, or products beyond the life of this book.

ISBN 978-1-4002-1352-8 (eBook)
ISBN 978-1-4002-1351-1 (TP)

Library of Congress Control Number: 2019938091

Printed in the United States of America

19 20 21 22 23   LSC   10 9 8 7 6 5 4 3 2 1

For my children, Lively, Sophia, and Benjamin, who have been my most faithful supporters, second only to their dad. May you have the courage and confidence to build satisfying and sturdy friendships in every season of your lives.

Contents

Introduction

We Need the Real Thing

The Mexican restaurant we had just arrived at made me nervous. My husband, Jimmy, had a concert to perform that night, and our gracious hosts had decided to honor our Texas heritage by taking us to their favorite south-of-the-border spot. The problem? We were in Nebraska.

Don't get me wrong, I love Mexican food. I was raised on the stuff. Give me some tender beef fajitas and fresh house-made guacamole, and I'm a happy girl. My problem with the Nebraska place was not that I didn't like Mexican food. It was that I *loved* it. As a native Houstonian, I was spoiled by the good stuff. And I had enough experience to know that any Mexican place north of Dallas would likely disappoint.

As expected, the food that night wasn't great. But our friends sincerely believed it was, and they waited eagerly for our approval. I'm not sure what we said to avoid exposing our subpar experience, but we tried our best not to offend. They just didn't know good Mexican food. Their version was merely Mexican*ish*.

This is a book about friendship. And, like with Mexican food, I only want the good stuff. The gift of friendship has produced some of the sweetest joys I've ever known. It has saved me from despair, given me courage to do things I never dreamed possible, comforted me in grief and loss, and sheltered me in the storms of suffering. I don't just like friendship; I *love* it.

By God's unfathomable mercy, I've been raised on the good stuff. I've had great friendships from a young age, and mercifully some of my closest friends began following Jesus around the same time I did. I experienced depths of camaraderie before the age of thirty that many people wait their whole lives for. It is because of my profound love for friendship that I am so dissatisfied with anything less than the best— anything merely friend-*ish*.

At some point, I began to look at the friendships of those around me and I was, frankly, shocked. Like stepping into that Nebraskan Mexican restaurant, my exposure to many Christians' versions of friendship produced disappointment and a longing for them to experience the real thing. So I began to write. In those early days of writing I realized many people had never tasted anything different. By tearing down inferior models, some accused me not only of ignorance but hatred of friendship. Nothing could be further from the truth. I love it so much that I only want the good stuff. For myself and for you. Let me prove it by sharing some of my friendship journey with you.

In 2009, I emailed a few women I knew to ask a simple question: Will you be my friend? After two moves and three years of touring with my musician husband, I realized I had no local friends. Sure, there were people I loved and cared for that I could call, but no friend I could drive down the street to see. I was starting a full-time ministry job and knew that long-distance friends wouldn't cut it. I needed someone physically present.

Brooke was the first to respond to my "I need friends" email, and for two years we met weekly at Starbucks. I began to meet other isolated Christians who were hungry for Jesus-centered companionship, so I rounded them up and the seven of us simply decided to be friends. We introduced ourselves, gave some details about our lives, and created a list of questions to ask ourselves every week, things like "How's your walk with God? How's your marriage? Are you putting your ministry, job, or family above Jesus?"

For the next couple of years we met every week. In that time there were ten pregnancies, four miscarriages, and six job losses between us and our husbands. Those years were hard, but we learned to be there out of a commitment to Christ and to one another. That season was terribly difficult and strikingly beautiful.

It was during this season that I faced my own crisis of faith. In the middle of an already difficult season, I miscarried for a third time. When that baby died, so did my faith, and I was left questioning who my God was.

One night, my friend Abbey and I found ourselves in our church's prayer room at the same time. When she asked me how I was, something inside me broke. I don't remember what she said to me or what she prayed for me. I just cried. I've never cried so hard in front of anyone the way I did with her that night. Her arm around my shoulder and her simple presence in that hard place was a balm to my soul. It was so sweet that words fail to do it justice. I'll never forget it. The Lord met me that night through her.

Friendship is an irreplaceable gift in the life of a Christian. Through it God encourages, consoles, and ministers kindness to us.

But this gift isn't always a healing balm; it can also be a war zone of conflict and hurt. In the midst of this already trying season, I was also wounded by a friend. Deeply wounded. And I didn't handle it well. Though I didn't see it then, I put up a wall in my heart toward her that day. Instead of responding with grace and forgiveness, I harbored my hurt and distanced myself from her. I was convinced we could never be close again.

But as God would have it, we were forced to continue life together in the same community. Instead of addressing the issue, I faked my way through it and said what I needed to say to keep peace. But with each avoidance of the truth, I was laying bricks on an already insurmountable wall in my heart. I played the role of a friend, but underneath, my heart grew bitter and distant.

Years (yes, years) into this relationship, I sensed the conviction of the Spirit. I began to see that avoiding conversations about the real problems and refusing to resolve the conflict was simply a form of selfishness in me. I preferred my own comfort over her well-being. I preferred fake friendship, because the real thing cost too much. So, I took a step forward and finally got honest with her. Initially, things got much worse. But slowly, through numerous hard, gut-wrenching, and awkward conversations, God brought breakthrough and restored a relationship that I once thought was irreparable.

Sarah is now one of my dearest friends, a precious sister in the faith, someone I long to share my heart with. I eagerly look forward to our time together. I wouldn't be who I am today without her.

Friendship is an irreplaceable gift in the life of a Christian. Through the hurts we experience, God exposes, changes, and sanctifies us.

But not all wounds are due to our friends' blindness and sin. Sometimes—if you're lucky—a friend will wound you in love to help you see your own blindness and sin. In 2015 I experienced what I can only describe as a spiritual depression. Though it was similar to the dark season of miscarriage, the role my friends played was very different. Instead of providing comfort, they shone a light on the dark corners of my life that didn't align with the truth. Holly was one of those friends.

She asked to meet with me one on one. We had just spent the weekend together with our families, and though it should have been a fun weekend, I spent most of it in the fog of my own hopelessness. So when she called me on the way home to schedule a one-on-one conversation, her tone of voice and the flavor of her words gave her away. Clearly, I had offended her, but, try as I might, I couldn't figure out how. So I showed up at our appointed time with anxiety in my heart.

Holly was aware of my current state of depression, yet she courageously and kindly exposed the self-centered attitude I was entrenched in but didn't yet have eyes to see. Yes, I was in a hard season. But, as her words helped me see, I was so consumed with my own troubles that I couldn't even recognize hers or anyone else's. A cancerous selfishness was growing behind my depression, hidden from my sight. Being a true friend, Holly couldn't stand by and say nothing. The moment was excruciating, but the clarity it brought allowed me to finally move past the mountain I had been circling for more than two years. Like the lancing of an infected wound, it hurt before it healed. You couldn't pay me enough to walk through that season again, but I wouldn't trade it for the world.

Friendship is an irreplaceable gift in the life of a Christian. Through it God deals death blows to our pride and selfishness. Without it, I'd still be circling that mountain in darkness.

Why share all of this?

To show you I am a product of great friendships. I am who I am today because of how God has used my friends in my life. In fact, you'll read many more stories from my own life and from my friends' lives as you journey through the pages of this book. Though I've changed all the names in this book, every story shared is real.

I love the gift of friendship. But I also want to let you know there are counterfeits, fraudulent forms of companionship not based on mutual love and affection. Instead, they're based solely on a self-centered craving to be loved. My hope is to give you a beautiful vision of true friendship and the ability to spot the fakes.

Most Christians aren't used to looking for counterfeit friendship. We assume friendship, even the world's version of it, is harmless. But the Bible doesn't treat any worldly philosophy as harmless. In Romans 12:2 we are commanded "not [to] be conformed to this world, but be transformed by the renewal of your mind." In Colossians 2:8 we are warned not to be taken "captive by philosophy and empty deceit, according to human tradition, according to the elemental spirits of the world, and not according to Christ." For the Christian, our friendships should not be according to the culture but according to Christ. Which, of course, begs the question, what is friendship according to Jesus? How does our faith affect our practice of this vital part of our lives? For many, all that their faith changes is the external trappings of their relationships. Instead of partying, we have Bible studies. Instead of clubbing, we host game nights. Instead of watching *50 Shades of Grey*, we watch *God's Not Dead*.

But is this God's goal, to simply turn drinking buddies into accountability partners? To turn gossip sessions into prayer requests? No! Far be it from us to expect so little transformation in our friendships! When the spiritually dead receive new life in Christ, the entire heartbeat of friendship is transformed. So let's fight for a biblical framework around our friendships, so we can enjoy the good stuff, and see with clarity the rising tide of philosophies presented in our culture. By gaining a vision of friendship according to Jesus, we will no longer need to settle for something merely friend-*ish*.

Digging in
Treasureless Fields

I met my friend Madison in second grade. We were both new to our school, though neither of us were new to being made fun of—me for ears that stuck out, Maddie for her British accent. So naturally we became best friends.

We braved our way through elementary and junior high together. We earned badges in Girl Scouts, carried our instruments together to orchestra, rode our bikes to each other's houses, and had sleepovers. And, because neither one of us were very cool, we accompanied each other to our eighth-grade dance, dateless.

But high school was a different ball game. By our sophomore year, Maddie quit playing violin, got a cool haircut, and started to meet new friends. I had always been the social butterfly of the two of us, so it was unusual for me to see her meeting new people. Others were starting to notice what I already knew: Madison was an incredibly sweet and kind person. Suddenly, I began to feel unsteady.

I remember my dilemma clearly. This was *my* best friend. I knew her best, better than all her new friends, not to mention her new boyfriend. I didn't want to share her with others. I wanted things to be how they always were. But I also knew I had no right to demand that of her. She wasn't mine. She didn't belong to me. Deep down, I knew I had to let her go. Let her make her own decisions. True love for my friend in this season looked like giving her space and being supportive from afar. And I didn't like it. It threw off my center of gravity. Suddenly, life felt unstable as things shifted in a relationship that had been in my life for a decade.

Friendships are tricky things, aren't they? They shift in unpredictable ways as we travel through life's many seasons. And because there's no rulebook, no clear-cut path or common set of expectations, friendships often feel unstable and fragile. Each close friend feels one life-stage change away from a distant memory. So we're left asking questions like, how will my friendships weather the transition from high school to college? Or, what should I expect when a good friend gets married and starts a family while I remain single? Or, what do I do now that my best friend just got the perfect job offer across the country? Should our friendships be free from obligation? Or should we be looking for covenant friendships? Is finding my tribe more important than finding my spouse?

Maybe we're asking more questions because we're confronted with the friendship issue more often. After all, friendship certainly seems to be buying up the cultural real estate. Need proof? This relationship called friendship is responsible for the emergence of at least two new holidays: Galentine's Day in February and Friendsgiving in November, both of which have become commercial product lines. With the largest population of singles in United States history, are we surprised?[1] Americans might not to be getting married and settling down, but we're still looking for a sense of community, belonging, and stability. And our gaze is turning to friends.

In 2017, Megan Gerber of *The Atlantic* made the same observation:

Friendships, increasingly, are playing an organizing role in society. Long conceived as side dishes to the main feast—marriage, kids, the nuclear family above all—friendships, more and more, are helping to define people's sense of themselves in the world. During a time of emergent adulthood and geographic mobility, friendships are lending stability—and meaning—to people's, and especially young people's, lives.[2]

Rebecca Traister, author of *All the Single Ladies*, agrees in her article "Girlfriends are the New Husbands":

But as mating patterns change, and many women put off marriage until their 30s, we gain a decade of independence; a decade that might once have been dedicated to bonding with husbands and children, but is now often unfettered by men or the limitations of family. We may be single, but rarely do we spend those years without a coterie of girlfriends. We may not be growing up within the context of our marriages anymore, but we are not alone. Women become each other's de facto spouses.[3]

A recent study of college men in the journal *Men and Masculinities* discovered this focus on friendship is not just a female thing. They found that male participants preferred intimate friendships with a male companion (a "bromance") over a romantic relationship with a woman, expressing that their "bromantic relationships were more satisfying in their emotional intimacy, compared to their heterosexual romances." One participant said, "Lovers are temporary; a bromance can last a lifetime."[4]

The authors of the study concluded this: "the bromance could increasingly become recognized as a genuine lifestyle relationship; whereby two heterosexual men can live together and experience all the benefits of a traditional heterosexual relationship."[5] To a world that doesn't want limitations or hindrances from sexual encounters, friendships now function as the stable family unit people still hunger for, while allowing them the sexual freedom they desire.

Not only is friendship the new family, but studies now show that this lifestyle of singleness actually promotes social connection better than marriage.[6] Bella DePaulo, also of *The Atlantic*, summarizes these findings:

> As many single people are realizing, adults don't need a spouse in the house to shield them from loneliness. The protections against loneliness are fairly straightforward: People who have more friends, or confidants to turn to in times of need, tend to be less lonely. And both single people and those who live alone tend to do equally well at cultivating friendships and maintaining ties with others.[7]

The Loneliness Epidemic

So if friendship, not marriage, is the antidote to loneliness, and friendship is more important than ever, shouldn't we be less lonely? Surprisingly, studies show the opposite is true. In 2017, former surgeon general Vivek Murthy declared a "loneliness epidemic" in the United States, stating that "loneliness and emotional well-being are serious public health concerns."[8]

In May 2018, Cigna released a study echoing Murthy's conclusion, citing that "only around half of Americans (53 percent) have meaningful in-person social interactions, such as having an extended conversation with a friend or spending quality time with family, on a daily basis."[9]

What's going on here?

Though Cigna highlighted several root causes, they focused on work-life balance: "There is an inherent link between loneliness and the workplace, with employers in a unique position to be a critical part of the solution." Do you feel lonely? Like you don't have good friendships? Apparently, your job may be to blame.

But that is just one of many explanations for why our friendships fail to satisfy us. Other explanations provided by our culture include: a lack of frientimacy (defined as the right balance of positivity, consistency, and vulnerability),[10] not prioritizing friendship enough,[11] mistakenly allowing marriage to be the centerpiece of human relationships,[12] an unwillingness to drop the act and show people our true selves,[13] failure to befriend the people we are most tempted to avoid,[14] or simply not exercising the right social skills to make friends.[15]

> Why don't our friendships satisfy us? Might I suggest it's because they were never meant to.

What is the real problem? Is it that we're working too hard? Or that we're being fake? Is it that we lack the right social skills or the right "frientimacy"? Though none of these suggestions are inherently wrong, they don't dig deep enough to hit the root of the problem.

Why don't our friendships satisfy us? Might I suggest it's because they were never meant to.

Right Desires, Wrong Field

We all want a friend who is consistent, a friend who is present, and a friend who values us. It's okay to admit it. I'm right there with you. In fact, our longing for this type of perfect friendship is something God wired into us. Just look around, and you'll see it.

The whole world is hunting for a perfect relationship. The search for such a love has been the centerpiece of endless books, songs, plays, and movies. And though its object comes in many forms—be it a spouse, a parent, a friend, or a lover—the longings underneath are ultimately the same: we're looking for someone we can commit to and who will commit to us, someone who will be present and available, someone who gives our life meaning, and someone who knows us and loves us fully. A perfect love that transcends all of life's trials and tribulations. A saving love.

But as soon as we search for this kind of love in friendship, or in any relationship for that matter, we find, like grasping at smoke, this goal quickly eludes us and often leaves us with more problems than when we first began.

This brings us to an important question: is it wrong to want stability, companionship, and significance? Is the desire itself wrong? Absolutely not! The problem is not *what* we are searching for but that we are searching for it in the *wrong place*.

In Jeremiah 2:13, God accuses his people of the same problem. Listen to his indictment: "For my people have committed two evils: they have forsaken me, the fountain of living waters, and hewed out cisterns for themselves, broken cisterns that can hold no water." The problem is not *that* the people were thirsty. The problem is *where* they went to satisfy their thirst.

Most of our problems in friendship are a result of searching for right things in the wrong places. We're digging for treasure in treasureless fields. No matter how hard we look, friendship will always turn up empty.

But there is a treasure to be found, a perfect love that transcends all of life's trials and tribulations. There is a relationship, a friendship, that *can* save us. Jesus affirms this in John 17:3: "And this is *eternal life, that they know you*, the only true God, and Jesus Christ whom you have sent."

Did you catch that? Jesus made it clear that eternal life is found in relationship. And it's not a relationship with our friends, with our spouses, or with our kids, but with God himself.

Again we see this same theme in 1 John 5:20: "And we know that the Son of God has come and has given us understanding, *so that we may know him who is true*; . . . [Jesus] is the true God and *eternal life*."

Eternal life is found in knowing God. Eternal life is not separate from God, as if it were a gift given by him. Eternal life *is* him. We were made for a perfect love that saves us, a love that stabilizes, a love that is present, and a love that gives us meaning. And it is found in only one person: Jesus Christ.

When we take these massive longings of our hearts and aim them at other people, we are sure to meet with disappointment. The most well-meaning people in the world will still fail to be consistent, present, and caring. We're all sinners. We fail. We make mistakes. We will disappoint each other. And we know it. Not one of us has met the perfect friend. Not one of us has been the perfect friend. Directing these desires at our friends is like trying to fill an ocean with a water dropper. I know, because I've tried.

The Search for Stability

When my friendship with Maddie began to change, sorrow and confusion came with it. Our friendship had been one of the pillars of my childhood, a safe place in the storms of puberty and junior high drama. But now that we were old enough to drive, I had to share her with all her new friends. I did my best to say goodbye to an old version of our friendship and timidly welcomed the new, but it was painful. Accepting changes in friendship is difficult, because, unlike with our family, there are no obligatory ties. It forces us into uncertainty, unsure of what is on the other side.

But is that how it's supposed to be?

Should our friendships be free from obligation? Should we have to hold them so open-handedly? There are many who answer that question with a resounding *no*. Entire books are being written, Christian and secular, arguing that we have the right to create obligations and commitments, even covenants, within our friendships. For many, friendships are the most important and consistent relationships in their lives. If friends are the new family, isn't it right that they should get the same public recognition? The same obligatory ties?

To answer these questions we must look to our only firm source of truth: the Bible. The Bible is clear about a lot concerning certain relationships: "Fathers, don't exasperate your children," "Children, obey your parents," "Wives, submit to husbands," "Husbands, love your wives," "Elders, shepherd the flock." But what about plain old friendships? Curiously, we find the Scriptures are largely quiet on this topic.

We know the Bible has a lot to say about friendship generally, like "love your neighbor as yourself and forgive one another as Christ forgave you." But, as I've studied the scriptures on this topic, I've found the Bible does not give any prescription or precedent for demanding a specific friend be our "friend forever" in the same way a man and woman become obligated to each other in marriage. Quite the opposite. In fact, we see many friends in the Bible parting ways as they seek to advance the Kingdom of God. So while some friends may choose to do life together for all of their years, we never have the right to demand or expect from friends what we might demand or expect from a spouse or parent. (If you're wondering what to do with the story of Jonathan and David covenanting together, see appendix 1.)

Don't mishear me; friendship should be an irreplaceable part of every Christian's life. In a way, friendship is more essential than marriage and family, because while not everyone will marry, everyone needs friends. But just because it is essential doesn't mean we should practice friendship in the same way we practice family.

So why is it that familial relationships get these obligations and friendship doesn't? The Bible tells us it's because marriage and family are shadows of greater and more important realities (John 1:12–13; Rom. 8:15–17; Eph. 5:31–32). The distinctions and obligations within these institutions are important because of the eternally good things they point to: union with Christ and the eternal family God adopts us into. We celebrate the obligatory nature of marriage and family, whether in our lives or others, out of love for Jesus and all that his blood has purchased for us. But a friendship is *not* a marriage; it is *not* a parent-child relationship. Therefore, it should not receive the same public recognition or obligatory ties.

So what are we to do when we experience shifts in our friendships like I did in tenth grade? How do we handle this instability? Do we fall back on marriage and family to stabilize us? What if we aren't married and don't have a stable family? What firm ground can we stand on?

Jesus, Our Stabilizer

While my friendship with Maddie was under construction, my prayer life skyrocketed. With my best friend being less available to me, I needed somewhere else to run. And by God's grace, I ran to Jesus. He became my consistent friend, my refuge, my stabilizer in all the changes. The instability in my friendship forced me to find stability in something else, in *someone* else.

Though I was tempted to demand things never change, doing so would likely have caused a bitter ending to our friendship. Because, ultimately, Madison could never have handled the pressure of being my refuge.

When our desire for stability is aimed at our friends, we naturally look for ways to create obligations, attempting to prevent future disruptions to the relationship. This may look like deciding to be roommates (because then they have to be my friend, at least for that year), starting a business together, joining a sports team together, or just making promises to each other to be there for life. Of course, I'm not saying that becoming roommates or business partners is bad. But when we do this with the purpose of tying a specific friend to ourselves, we are simply digging in a treasureless field. Not only will we never find the stability we're looking for, we're also only using our friend to get what we need. It's a self-centered version of friendship and therefore unacceptable for those who follow Jesus.

But when Jesus is our stability—our consistent friend and refuge—we are freed to truly love others and love them sacrificially. With Jesus as my stability, I found the strength to resist the pull toward bitterness and to continue loving Maddie through our final years of high school and into college. Through the ups and downs of those years, I learned how to lean more of my weight on Jesus and to be a true friend to her. I believe it's because of those difficult lessons that we're still good friends to this day.

The Search for Companionship

Jimmy and I got married when we were both twenty years old and his music career was just taking off. Going into marriage I assumed, as many do, that I'd never be lonely again! Marriage eradicates loneliness, right?

Wrong.

Two weeks into marriage I felt lonelier than I ever had before. Not because Jimmy wasn't around. He was. And not because Jimmy wasn't affectionate. He was. I was lonely because of my sin.

Marrying Jimmy exposed a lot of pride in my heart. Before we met, I felt confident in myself. I had a lot of friends and was generally well-liked by people. But when I began to travel with him, a new phenomenon happened: I became known only as Mrs. Needham.

People cared about me because of who I was married to. I was no longer receiving compliments about me but about him: "Your husband is so amazing!" And honestly, he is amazing. But being sidelined didn't sit well with all that hidden pride lurking in my heart: *Excuse me,* I thought, *I'm awesome too! I have things to offer too! He's not the only special one here.*

I remember sitting in a hotel room in Nashville in the middle of a promotional tour for his upcoming record, wondering what had gone wrong. I felt so alone. So isolated and forgotten. But sitting next to me was the most kind, patient, and loving man I had ever met. Clearly loneliness is not just an issue of having loving people around you. In my situation, I was lonely because I was still holding onto my pride. My sin was separating me from God and from my husband. The proof? I didn't want to talk to either of them.

In those first few months of marriage, I aimed my aching loneliness at Jimmy, demanding that he eradicate it with better words and better actions. "Why haven't you said you loved me yet today?" "How come you didn't mention me on stage?" "Am I even important to you?" Demands spilled out of my mouth daily as I desperately tried to rid myself of the sinking feeling of isolation. But no matter how often and how frequently he professed his love for me, I continued to feel alone.

In addition to my incurable loneliness, I became utterly self-centered in my marriage. So long as I assumed my husband was my savior from the loneliness, I was unable to love and serve him the way God called me to.

Though I'm using my marriage as an example here, I've seen the same principle play itself out in friendships. As soon as we see our friends as the solution to our loneliness, we cease to be able to love them sacrificially.

Jesus, Our Companion

We often assume our feelings of loneliness exist because we don't have enough people in our lives. And even if we do, we assume they aren't the right kind of people. Surely there are more loving, thoughtful, caring people out there who would instinctively know when to reach out.

But I can tell you from my own experience that having the best friends, family, and church within your reach still won't resolve your loneliness if you're unwilling to deal with the sin in your own life. Loneliness is not primarily a people problem but an unbelief problem; it's an unwillingness to turn to God to meet our souls' deepest needs.

We see this concept play out in the first few chapters of Genesis. Though Adam was alone in the Garden, he was not lonely. He had perfect fellowship with God. Compare that to Adam's post-sin condition. After their forbidden-fruit tasting, Adam and Eve willingly withdrew from God by hiding from him, and they withdrew from one another by pointing fingers. Adam was no longer alone, but he was lonely. Sin separates. Sin destroys fellowship. Sin creates loneliness.

Paul Tripp explained this phenomenon with insightful accuracy:

> Sin is fundamentally antisocial, because sin causes me to love me more than anything else and to care for me more than anything else. Living for myself and the satisfaction of my selfish desires dehumanizes the people in my life. No longer are they people to me. No longer are they objects of my affection and service. No, my loved ones and friends are reduced either to vehicles to help me get what I want or to obstacles in the way of what I want.[16]

If sin is the cause of our loneliness, then Christ, not a human relationship like friendship, is the solution. Not only is he the solution to free us from our sin, he is the only one who can fully satisfy all our longings for companionship and our desire to have someone always present and available.

Things changed in my marriage when I began to turn away from my sin and turn back to God. I stopped searching for perfect companionship in the field of marriage and recognized God as my only never-failing companion. Loneliness was eradicated when I made my relationship with God right. Once I began to draw near to him again, in humility and repentance, he fulfilled his promise and drew near to me (James 4:6–8). And as God became my closest friend again, I was freed to truly love and enjoy my husband and be the support he needed me to be.

> Loneliness is not primarily a people problem but an unbelief problem; it's an unwillingness to turn to God to meet our souls' deepest needs.

The Search for Significance

Nothing throws a wrench in your friendships like moving to a new city. All those familiar questions from junior high pop up again: "Will they like me? Does everyone here already have their own friends? Will I fit in?"

Having spent most of my life in the Houston area, I moved to a suburb of Dallas in 2011 with my husband. Thankfully we knew a few families there, and I started to build a relationship with Laci, the wife of another musician. She was a huge answer to prayer! She had space in her life to build a new friendship and was eager to seek God, so we began to meet weekly to study the book of Job and pray together.

One day, I texted her to see if she wanted to hang out. She graciously declined, explaining that she was spending time with another friend, someone we both knew.

A sea of insecurities hit me as I remembered that I was the new friend. Laci already had established friendships, and ours was still forming. Maybe she was just humoring me—the new girl in town—by meeting with me. I questioned whether our friendship was as strong as I thought. Where did I stand with her? If she made a list of her closest friends, would I be on it?

This wouldn't be the first time I wondered about my standing with someone. I'm sure you can relate. From the friendship bracelets of junior high, to the MySpace "top 8" of high school (shout out to my thirty-somethings out there), to the birthday party and bridal shower invitations (or lack thereof), underneath it all we're wondering, *How important am I? Do I matter? Am I significant?*

These questions are not new. In fact, we see Jesus' friends asking the same question on more than one occasion. In Luke 22:24 he tells us, "A dispute also arose among them, as to which of them was to be regarded as the greatest."

That dispute might strike some people as silly, but not me. This moment seems so plausible, so similar to how we think about our friend-ships. I imagine Peter reminding the disciples that Jesus called him the rock and John pointing out how many times he leaned against Jesus at mealtimes. We're all eager to know, *Do I matter? Am I most important?*

A young man in my church recently told me of his own struggle with this: "I often compare my friendship with my friend to his friendship with other guys. I will compare the way that he and I interact to the way he interacts with his other male friends. Does he seem to have as much fun with me as he does with his other 'bros'? Is our friendship as enriching to him as his other friendships are? I feel that I need to be his best friend in order to feel okay about myself."

Social media has only aggravated our condition, because we now have a tool to spy on the activity of others and see how we measure up. We can spend every waking moment obsessing about our own sig-nificance by measuring it against those around us. Do we have better friends? More friends? Are we someone's best friend?

Jesus, Our Significance

The disciples had it wrong. And so do we. When we aim our longing for significance at people, we end up using people like a ladder, seeing how many rungs we can climb to get to the top. How many people can we beat out at being someone's best friend? We all want to be significant to someone. We all want to be the greatest in some way.

With my friend Laci, so long as I was obsessed about where I stood with her, I couldn't love her well. When I became aware of my self-centered thoughts, I did the only thing I knew to do. I got down on my knees in my kitchen where I had just received her "rejection" text and began to pray. For her. I asked God to give both of them a joyful time together. I asked him to encourage them and strengthen the bonds of their friendship. And I begged God to remind me of what I knew in my head but had forgotten in my heart: that knowing he loved me was all the significance I needed.

Whether Laci actually counted me among her close friends didn't matter quite as much once I drew near to God. His love for me changed my perspective. He helped me see the opportunity I had to love and serve her for as long as she was in my life. And finding my worth in knowing Jesus was the only thing that enabled me to love her that way.

When Suffering Deepens Our Longings

Sometimes it isn't just our own misdirected longings at play. The things we've suffered at the hands of other people can intensify and complicate our longings.

For example, God designed the family to be a basic experience of stability and consistency in our lives as we grow up. But for many people, this is something they had to do without. Whether your parents divorced, were never married, or your home was simply an unsafe place, your family might have been the opposite of dependable. This forces children to find constancy outside of the home in their most formative years. For many, their friends become that consistent refuge. The loss of a safe family environment only intensifies the longing for stability.

Physical, sexual, and emotional abuse take a severe toll on these longings as well. What should have been a good thing, closeness to another person, is turned into a nightmare. Though the longing for companionship with others may still exist, these wounds attach fear and distrust to them. When a safe person is found, it's tempting to cling to them and demand they never leave for fear such a person will never be found again.

The same is true with any other form of suffering. Whether it is the betrayal of a friend, the loss of a loved one, or having physical disabilities or pain, all that we suffer can complicate our longings and justify the temptation we already have to look to people, not God, for our primary relational needs. Our suffering ought to turn us toward God, but our default is to turn toward each other.

> If we look to specific people to be our hope and lifeline, our only way to heal, our only source of comfort, then we have elevated a grace of God into the place of God.

I don't want to downplay the important role people have in our healing. God often meets us in suffering through the hands of other people: the local church, counselors, friends, family. But these people are not and can never be our savior in the hardship. If we look to specific people to be our hope and lifeline, our only way to heal, our only source of comfort, then we have elevated a grace of God into the place of God.

I cannot address these issues in-depth here, nor do I mean to. But it's important to at least make you aware that the suffering you've experienced may be shaping how you approach friendship. If you've never done so, I hope you'll seek the Lord for healing and reach out to biblical counselors and find other resources that address these situations biblically.[17]

Enemies in Disguise

As Christians, we know that friendship (what we often call community) is vital to our emotional and spiritual health. It is unequivocally a good thing, a precious gift from God. But we also must acknowledge that friendship is only that: one of God's gifts, not God himself. And like everything that is not the fountain of living water, friendship will always be a broken cistern, something that has no ability to quench the deep thirst in our souls.

And this is the heartbeat behind Christian friendship. It is companionship forged in the fire of the conviction that Jesus alone can satisfy our souls. Jesus is our Bread of Life, our Living Water, our Pearl of Great Price, our Light, our Resurrection, our very Life. The greatest danger to our souls is that we might abandon abiding in him, following him, and finding our joy in him. Therefore, the best gift a friend can give is a commitment to fight alongside us for our joy in and communion with Christ.

Conversely, the worst distortion of friendship arises when a friend encourages us, consciously or unconsciously, to place our affections elsewhere. The apostle Peter unwittingly acts out this kind of distortion in Matthew 16. Jesus tells his disciples that he will die and rise again (v. 21). Peter rebukes Jesus with what was surely a well-intentioned comment from a loyal friend: "Far be it from you, Lord! This shall never happen to you" (v. 22).

It looks like the deepest, most genuine, most beautiful form of friendship, but Peter's words put him between Jesus and Jesus' obedience to the Father. His ignorance made a friend into an enemy, at least for a moment. "Get behind me, Satan! You are a hindrance to me" (v. 23). What Peter thought was helpful, Jesus called a hindrance. What Peter assumed was godly friendship, Jesus called satanic opposition.

So as we dive deep into what godly friendship really is, we must learn to identify these enemies in disguise, these counterfeit friendships that appear good, even godly. My hope is to show you what makes friendship truly precious and give you the courage and confidence to build friendships that quicken your desires for God and promote dependency on Jesus, not on one another. You'll see that when we find all we need in Christ, we will be free to truly love our friends, not use them to meet our needs.

Marks of a Counterfeit:
Replacing Jesus

F or the last six months, I have been easily depressed and very sensitive to the lack of love my friends have been showing me," Kara
told me. Her life had been unusually difficult as of late, and as we
shared a meal together the subject of expectations in friendship came
up. "Every other week I would focus on a different friend and evaluate if I felt loved by them. I would notice if they didn't show me the
care I wanted and begin to wonder if they ever loved me at all. I kept
track of how often they texted me back, if they asked how I was doing
or remembered things going on in my life. I fixated on how I wasn't
enough or—worse—how they weren't good enough friends, and this
tempted me to retaliate by ignoring them."

Kara had a real need to be unconditionally loved and cared for. But instead of turning to Jesus, the only one who could truly meet her need, she had turned to friendship and was met with disappointment.

Preston told me a similar story about his friendships. When he first became a Christian, he prayed earnestly for godly friendships to help him as he grew in his faith. Eventually, the Lord answered and provided many friends, but two in particular, Josh and David, became especially dear to him. "We were like the three musketeers but without the swords and swashbuckling garb. After a couple of years, though, I noticed feelings of jealousy and anxiety whenever Josh and David got together without me. I feared I would be left behind as they grew closer.

"One night, at our church's small-group gathering, I overheard them talking together about Josh's insecurities about the future. It confirmed all my fears that I was indeed being left out, and I lost it. Though I was literally surrounded by good friends in that moment, I felt overcome with loneliness, fear, and jealousy. I couldn't even focus on the conversations I was having with the people right in front of me. It was after this night that I realized Josh and David had become idols in my heart. Instead of letting these friendships point me to Jesus, I had let them replace Jesus."

Like me, Preston and Kara had also tried digging for treasure in the treasureless field of friendship. They let their friendships play roles only Jesus should play. And when friendship attempts to take Jesus' place, it's not real friendship. It's a counterfeit.

Friendship Is Important

It's not that friendship isn't important. It is. Where would David be without Jonathan? Would Naomi have survived without Ruth's devotion? How different would Paul's ministry have been without the comfort and camaraderie of Timothy? Everywhere we look in the Bible, we see friendship matters.

I'm not sure where you're coming from as you read this book. You might already be pursuing deeper friendships. Maybe you want to but are unsure where to start. Or maybe you have a deep resistance to the idea of friendship. It may be a reaction to past abuse, when your vulnerability was used to harm you. It may be from past rejection, when your pursuit of friendship caused deeper isolation and hurt. Maybe you were betrayed by a friend, or were bullied by those you thought you could trust. All these things can turn us off to the idea of drawing near to another person.

But just because we *can* do life on our own doesn't mean we should. Our calling is a corporate one. Following Jesus is an individual decision, but not an individual assignment. We are a chosen race, not a chosen person. We are a royal priesthood, not a royal priest. We are a holy nation, a people for his own possession. We are not on this journey by ourselves.

As Paul described to the Corinthian church, we are "those sanctified in Christ Jesus, called to be saints *together* with all those who in every place call upon the name of our Lord Jesus Christ, both their Lord and ours" (1 Cor. 1:2).

Jesus modeled this togetherness in his time on earth. Though he was God and needed nothing from mankind, he chose to live out his obedience in the company of friends. He brought them into very personal and intimate moments of his life, even though it brought him great harm. His friends betrayed him, allowing him to be physically abused and beaten and killed. They permitted his bullying by the religious elite and often didn't step in to defend him. They fell asleep at his greatest hour of need, and most ran away after his unjust arrest. Jesus has the scars that being friends with sinners brings. Even so, he valued friendship and so must we.

My friend Preston was right to pray for godly friendships. Friendship is indeed vital in our lives. But, as vital as friendship is, it is not ultimate.

Friendship Is Secondary

Friendship was originally God's idea. From walking with Adam and Eve in the cool of the day in Genesis to making his dwelling with us in Revelation, God's plan has always been to befriend mankind.

But, as Isaiah reminded us, "our iniquities have made a separation between you and your God, and your sins have hidden his face from you so that he does not hear" (Isa. 59:2). How can sinners be friends with a holy and just God? How will God reconcile sinners back into fellowship with him?

The answer: at great cost to himself.

This friendship we have with God is an expensive one. It is through the humble incarnation, the perfect obedience, the costly death, and the resurrection of Jesus that God reconciled us to himself. In Jesus we are saved. In Jesus we are reconciled to God. In Jesus we have a truly saving friendship.

But there's a catch: Jesus is not content being one among our many friends. In Luke 14:26 he declares that "if anyone comes to me, and does not hate his own father and mother and wife and children and brothers and sisters, yes, and even his own life, he cannot be my disciple." Jesus demands our ultimate loyalty, to be our friend above all others. Our devotion to him should be so paramount that all other affections look like hate by comparison. Either Jesus is first in our life or he is not in our life.

Other New Testament authors affirm this need for ultimate loyalty. Paul, writing to the Corinthians, said, "But I am afraid that as the serpent deceived Eve by his cunning, your thoughts will be led astray from *a sincere and pure devotion to Christ*" (2 Cor. 11:3).

To the Romans, Paul defined sin as a preference for created things (or people) over the Creator: "they exchanged the truth about God for a lie and worshiped and *served the creature rather than the Creator*, who is blessed forever!" (Rom. 1:25).

And in Philippians we hear the echo of Jesus' words in Paul's personal confession:

> But whatever gain I had, I counted as loss for the sake of Christ. Indeed, *I count everything as loss because of the surpassing worth of knowing Christ Jesus my Lord.* For his sake I have suffered the loss of all things and count them as rubbish, in order that I may gain Christ. (Phil. 3:7–8)

This is not only a New Testament concept. From the earliest moments in the Bible, God demands our ultimate loyalty. We see this when God tells Abraham to sacrifice his only son, the very son God himself promised and provided. Would Abraham be loyal to God or to God's gifts? Once it was evident that Abraham planned to go through with it, God stopped him: "Do not lay your hand on the boy or do anything to him, for now I know that you fear God, seeing you have not withheld your son, your only son, from me" (Gen. 22:12).

What is acted out in Abraham's life is put into law on Mount Sinai: "You shall have no other gods before me" (Ex. 20:3).

And upon entering the Promised Land, God's primary reminder to his people is that their highest loyalty belongs to him alone:

> Hear, O Israel: The LORD is our God, the LORD is one. You shall love the LORD your God with all your heart and with all your soul and with all your might. And these words that I command you

today shall be on your heart. You shall not go after other gods, the gods of the peoples who are around you. (Deut. 6:4–6, 14)

God—God alone—is to receive our highest affections. This is not a suggestion. This is life and death for God's people. Later in Deuteronomy we see the severe consequences of letting other people compete with God's place:

> If your brother, the son of your mother, or your son or your daughter or the wife you embrace or *your friend who is as your own soul* entices you secretly, saying, "Let us go and serve other gods," which neither you nor your fathers have known, some of the gods of the peoples who are around you, whether near you or far off from you, from the one end of the earth to the other, you shall not yield to him or listen to him, nor shall your eye pity him, nor shall you spare him, nor shall you conceal him. But you shall kill him. Your hand shall be first against him to put him to death, and afterward the hand of all the people. (Deut. 13:6–9)

Obviously, we are not living under Old Testament law anymore; however, this passage still showcases an important part of God's character: he will not endure our divided affections, regardless of how special the people are with whom we divide them. For the Christian, it is either God first and God alone or not at all. He will not settle for second or even share first place.

That good things can become ultimate is not a new concept. The best things in life often pose the greatest threat to our undivided devotion to God. Tim Keller says it this way in his book *Counterfeit Gods*: "We think that idols are bad things, but that is almost never the case. The greater the good, the more likely we are to expect that it can satisfy our deepest needs and hopes. Anything can serve as a counterfeit god, especially the best things in life."[1]

As soon as a friendship begins to foster dependence on and loyalty to one another above Christ, it becomes dangerous. As soon as a friend is meeting needs in us only God should meet, it becomes idolatry. As soon as a friendship loses the ability to lovingly point out the sin that keeps us from Jesus, it becomes a hindrance, not a help. As soon as we put ourselves at the center of friendship, we have misused friendship altogether.

John Piper describes the paradox of Christian friendship this way: "On the one hand I say, I need you. God has appointed you as a means of grace to help me endure to the end. But on the other hand, I must say that the only way you can really help me is by saying something or doing something that will cause me to depend on God and not you."[2]

The best things in life often pose the greatest threat to our undivided devotion to God.

Friendship is an irreplaceable gift of God. But like all of God's gifts, it matters that we receive and enjoy it God's way. Sex is a good gift from God, but only when enjoyed in marriage. Wealth is a good gift from God, but only when free from greed. And friendship is a good gift from God, but only when it fosters and preserves devotion to our One True Friend. It must always come second.

Rightly Ordered Loves

It's not that we don't need friends. God created us for community. Truly, it is not good for us to be alone. But ultimately, our community points us to something better, to God himself: the Communal Three-in-One, Father, Son, and Holy Spirit. Yes, we desperately need healthy, intimate, godly friends. But even good and necessary things can be inflated beyond their intended purpose and overshadow the God to whom they point.

So what are we to do? Are we to love people less? Or course not! The takeaway is not to stop loving but to keep our loves rightly ordered. Specifically, as we talked about earlier, God should not be one of many things we love. He ought to be the greatest thing we love. The recipient of our highest loyalties, our deepest affections, and our greatest dependency. Only when God occupies first place in our lives can we truly love our friends appropriately.

As I discussed this idea with my friend Shelby, she recounted her own friendship problems growing up. Like most kids, she longed to be in the popular crowd. But by the time she was in seventh grade, her desire to be included in this exclusive group of girls had become an obsession. At the time, she had only one friend, Julie, who was as faithful as they come. They were neighbors and had been good friends for years, often spending every weekend together.

One day, the popular girls called Shelby over and literally asked her point-blank: "Do you want to be popular like us? Do you want to be our friend?" She couldn't believe it! Finally, her dreams were coming true! They continued, "There's only one condition: you can't be friends with Julie anymore." This was a high cost for Shelby. But it was a cost she willingly accepted in exchange for entrance into the tribe she was sure would fulfill her.

Of course, it didn't bring fulfillment. Soon after selling out Julie, the girls turned on her, telling her it had been a joke. So began Shelby's experience of years of bullying that followed her until graduation. Despite this, she continued to do all she could to gain entry into these "fulfilling" friendships. She starved herself to be pretty enough and became a flirt to land a boyfriend and boost her status.

Looking back, she told me, "I still grieve the pain I caused Julie that day. She was a faithful, kind, and true friend, and I betrayed her. More than that, I grieve my sin of seeking fulfillment in those friendships instead of Jesus."

It was a deeper relationship with Jesus that finally dethroned her desire to be friends with the "important" people. Had this happened earlier in her life, she might have been able to be the kind of faithful friend to Julie that Julie had been to her.

Putting Jesus first doesn't cause us to love people less; rather, our devotion to him frees us from using friends to meet our needs and enables us to truly love them.

Signs of Idolatry

So how can we tell if a friendship has replaced Jesus in our lives? We have to start by looking at the roles only Jesus should have and work backward from there.

Jesus Is Our Savior.

When we were helpless, dead in our trespasses and sins, he brought us to life. Through his death and resurrection he did the work we couldn't do. We were lifeless, and he was and is our lifeline. Our need for him as savior isn't a one-time event. Every time we find ourselves drowning, helpless to do what we know we must do, he is our savior. Through the help of his Spirit in us, he does for us what we cannot do for ourselves. He is daily our lifeline. The one who comes through for us.

But sometimes our friends can seem more dependable than Jesus in this role. We can see them, talk to them, and physically hold onto them. In moments of need and helplessness, if our first action step is to reach out for a friend before we reach out to Jesus, it's a problem. Don't misunderstand me, friends are a key part of the fight of faith. I often ask friends to remind me of the truth that Jesus is an able savior for what I am facing. But this is different than looking to a friend to pull us out of the pit. When a friend seems like a more competent savior than Jesus, something is wrong.

Jesus Is Our Mediator.

Without him, we cannot be reconciled to God. Without him, we cannot draw near to God. Without him, we cannot have a relationship with God. Jesus alone can close the gap. So when we feel unable to grow closer to God without a particular friend, they've become too inflated. If a friend becomes our connection with God, the primary means by which we draw near to him, we have elevated him or her too high. There is only one mediator between God and man, and it is not your friend. It is the man Jesus Christ (1 Tim. 2:5).

Jesus Is Our Shepherd.

He guides us and leads us. He directs us and protects us. We are the sheep of his pasture. If we feel unable to make decisions without the direction of a friend, we've gone to the wrong shepherd. If we feel paralyzed without the affirmation of a friend, we've gone to the wrong protector. If we are unable to move forward and take risks unless a certain friend is by our side as our safe place, we've allowed a friend to play a role that only Jesus can fill.

This does not mean there is no place for mentors. It is good to seek the counsel and wisdom of those who are a few steps ahead of us. It is normal to need and seek discipleship from other mature believers. But good mentors should cultivate our dependence on Christ, not on themselves. Good mentors don't replace Jesus; they point to him.

Jesus Is Our Satisfaction.

Jesus told us he is the bread of life and living water. He told us we cannot come to him unless we are willing to eat his flesh and drink his blood. What can he mean by that? Obviously, we cannot literally do this. The point is this: Jesus is for our souls what food and water are for our bodies. He is our sustenance and satisfaction. He is what we need to spiritually thrive. He is what we need to feel complete, fulfilled, and satisfied.

So it is alarming when any other person produces these thoughts in us: *I cannot live without you. Talking with you is my lifeline. Our friendship is what I need to thrive.* If you are not okay without your friend, if going a day without talking is too long, then you are looking to that friendship as your soul's bread and water, your daily internal sustenance.

Jesus Is Our Judge.

His verdict is the only one that matters. His courtroom is the only one that can actually justify us or condemn us. This means his opinion of us is the only one that matters. Paul describes this in 1 Corinthians 4:3–4: "But with me it is a very small thing that I should be judged by you or by any human court. In fact, I do not even judge myself. . . . It is the Lord who judges me." Paul knew that in the courtroom of Christ, he stood justified by faith in front of the most important person in the world, so what did it matter what other people thought of him?

When we allow our friends to play the role of judge in our life, we live for their approval. We are constantly comparing our lives to others, wondering where we stack up and how our friends see us.

My friend Tyler experienced the temptation to look to a friend as judge when he was in college: "There was a guy in one of my classes who was funny and well-liked. I envied and craved the approval he got from our classmates and thought I could achieve that same level of public approval if I could simply earn his. If I said something funny and he laughed, I felt like I was in right standing with everyone. Conversely, if I perceived he didn't like me or didn't approve of my behavior, I felt like I was good for nothing. In that season, I lived or died by his approval. Though I couldn't see it or articulate it then, he had become both judge and savior to me."

We've all been there, longing for the approval of one specific friend or group of friends. Hoping they'll notice us, accept us, and approve of us. So the question is, why is it so difficult to quit this game? Why doesn't God's approval of us affect us the way it did Paul, liberating us from obsessing over our station in life? The Bible's answer to that question is this: we love the glory that comes from man more than the glory that comes from God.

In John 12 we read about some Jewish higher-ups who, like us, loved the glory of man: "Nevertheless, many even of the authorities believed in [Jesus], but for fear of the Pharisees they did not confess it, so that they would not be put out of the synagogue; for they loved the glory that comes from man more than the glory that comes from God" (John 12:42–43).

These men in authority had the same problem we do: they loved their status in the synagogue. They loved being in the "in" crowd—being important in their human circles—and they knew that following Jesus would strip it all away. And did you notice the reason for this? "They loved the glory that comes from man more than the glory that comes from God." Like these men, we are tempted to *love* human glory. To *love* the praise of people. To *love* to be made much of. The glory of man is often far more attractive to us than the glory offered to us by becoming children of God. The easiest way to see this in our hearts is when we constantly compare ourselves to others and incessantly crave approval from our peers. This is how we can know we're letting our friends replace Jesus as judge in our lives: when we prefer their glory to his.

And Finally, Jesus Is Our Boast.

A simple way to see if a friend is replacing Jesus in your life is to notice how often you talk about them. In 1 Corinthians 1:30 it says, "Jesus has become for us sanctification, redemption, wisdom from God so that he who boasts boasts in the Lord." When Jesus is our savior, our shepherd, our mediator, and our satisfaction, we boast about him. We talk about whatever is filling these roles in our lives. So who are you bragging about? Who is most often on your lips? Out of the heart the mouth speaks.

But it's not just that we allow others to replace Jesus in our lives; sometimes *we enjoy being Jesus* to someone else. One of the men on staff at our church shared that he understood this temptation. "Years ago a friend asked me to be his accountability partner. We met weekly to confess sin and apply the Gospel to his situation. Soon, there were big changes in him as a result of God's work and our intentional pursuit of seeing this sin destroyed. Though it was God at work in him, I began to see myself as the key to his change. I purposely put myself in positions where he would continue to see me as a wise person with the right answers and the secrets to change. I began to crave the affirmation and respect he gave me. At the time, I couldn't see it, but I was chasing the credit owed to the Lord because of my own savior complex."

It can feel great to be needed, to be essential to someone else's existence, to know that you matter because your friend cannot thrive without you. Being highly esteemed by one person is often more attractive than being esteemed by many people. Or it is at least a good alternative if popularity proves to be hard to come by. But hear this: it is sinful to act like a savior to other people. As Paul said in 1 Corinthians 3:6–7, "I planted, Apollos watered, but God gave the growth. So neither he who plants nor he who waters is anything, but only God who gives the growth."

How can we tell if this is us? When we begin to think things like, *I'm the only one who can help her. He needs me. No one else understands him the way I do.* Or we may enjoy being Jesus to others if the only people we befriend are people we can help, and we avoid befriending people who don't seem to need anything from us.

In summary, we know a friendship is replacing Jesus when:

- A friend is our *savior*, seeming to be more dependable and trustworthy than Jesus. When they are the first or only person we reach to for help, even before we pray. When a specific friend is the only one who can help us, and no other Christian friend will do.

- A friend is our *mediator*, becoming necessary for us to feel close to God. When they become required for our relationship with God to thrive.
- A friend is our *shepherd*, the only one we trust to help us make decisions.
- A friend is our *satisfaction*, becoming necessary for our soul's joy and happiness.
- A friend is our *judge*, the one whose opinion we obsess about and look to for ultimate approval.
- A friend is who we *boast* about more than Christ, constantly bragging on and praising them. When we are more thankful for that friend than we are thankful for Jesus.
- We *enjoy being Jesus* to others and so see no reason to befriend someone who doesn't have a need for us. Or we enjoy being the only person who can help, feeling threatened when others in the community step up to help.

Idolatry: A Less Than Popular Diagnosis

If you feel resistant to what you just read I wouldn't be surprised. Idolatrous friendships are not only normative in our culture, they're celebrated as *best* friendships. To the world, a best friend is *supposed* to fill these roles in your life. If two friends can't function without each other, it's not a cause for concern but for celebration that you found your BFF. If she's the only friend who can help you or he's the only one you can be yourself around, that's not alarming. It's simply a sign you're best friends. It's no wonder that so many people feel insecure if they do not have a best friend, as if they are missing out on some important life experience. Having a BFF is as important as having a significant other nowadays

Another reason for our resistance is that these friendships, at least in the beginning, feel like winning the friendship jackpot. Like you've finally found the person who gets you, who is there for you, and who makes you feel at home. When our idol has not yet failed us, when the water has not yet drained out of the broken cistern, when the storm has not yet come to destroy our house built on sand, we perceive our friendship to be the best thing ever. But just because a friendship that replaces Jesus "feels right" does not make it right.

We live in a world that rejects the existence of sin. The idea that the things we do and the things we prefer could be inherently wrong is appalling to most. There's only one problem: sin *does* exist. And rejecting its existence doesn't spare you from its consequences. Like a homeowner rejecting the reality of a leak in the roof, eventually you'll have to invent an explanation for the wet floor.

> Just because a friendship that replaces Jesus "feels right" does not make it right.

Eventually, our worship of friendship will cause problems, and then we'll be looking for answers. But who wants to hear that idolatry is the problem? Who wants to hear that it's our own sinful hearts at fault? We'd rather believe the floor is wet because a glass was spilled than believe the roof is leaking. If something's been spilled, the remedy is only a towel, while a busted roof requires gutting parts of the house and rebuilding from the inside out. And who wants to deal with that?

Yes, the truth hurts sometimes, but it will always set us free. Every time. And the truth is, letting our friends play roles only Jesus should is sin.

Unfortunately, many Christians don't have a category for a sinful friendship, especially a same-sex friendship. This false sense of security is the reason many have walked into idolatry without a second thought: they assumed a Christian friend could never be an idol. And they are blindsided when something eventually threatens their relationship and sends them spiraling.

I received an email from a young man describing this very experience:

> I have a close friend at church, who I've considered my best friend. About a year and a half ago I overheard him talking with someone about missing another friend, and for some reason it caught me off guard. Later that day I had an extreme amount of anxiety about what he said. This was surprising, since I've never experienced that kind of emotion before in my life and I was clueless about what to do. I started becoming emotionally dependent on my encounters with him and his claims of us always being best friends.

Far too many of us pursue friendship, because our souls are thirsty for something only Jesus can provide. We're longing for someone to love us, to make us feel important, to be there no matter what. But when we choose to take our longings to friends instead of Christ, it isn't real friendship. When we come thirsty, we simply end up using our friends to serve ourselves. A thirsty soul is a greedy soul, causing us to enter friendship as a consumer, looking for what we can get instead of what we can give. This self-love is the second mark of counterfeit friendship and what we'll look at next.

Marks of a Counterfeit: Selfishness

I had just sat down in Spanish class when the most popular girl in eighth grade walked into the room, her face peeking out behind a mountain of flowers. It was her birthday and, as was tradition in our school, all of her many friends and admirers had brought her bouquets of fresh blooms.

It was a strange tradition for a junior high school, but it did accomplish an important junior high objective: establishing a hierarchy of popularity. The more flowers you had on your birthday, the more important you were. Simple.

Though my friends and I weren't in the coveted cool crowd, we still joined in the flower-giving festivities as each of our birthdays came around. Seeing as it was my last year in junior high, I decided to step it up a notch. I generously gave flowers to as many friends as I could, even those I wasn't particularly close to. I relished in my own thoughtfulness. What a good friend I was!

Soon my own birthday approached. A few days before I turned fourteen, I silently tallied up all the bouquets I had given that year. *Wow,* I thought, *I may get ten bouquets of flowers this time around!* I daydreamed about how popular I would look as I plopped my stack of carnations and roses down in each class throughout the day.

To my dismay, I only received a measly few. Instead of being grateful for the thoughtfulness of the few friends I did have, I wallowed in self-pity and regretted all my previous bouquet buys. My disappointment betrayed my generosity for what it was: utter selfishness. At the end of the day, I was giving to get.

This is nothing new. Since our departure from Eden, our ability to pervert good deeds with selfish motives has always been present. We see it in Saul's generous gift of his daughter in marriage to David, only to use it as a means to get him killed. We see it in Delilah's professions of love to Samson, only as a means to gain wealth. We see it in the Pharisees' generosity to God, only as a means to withhold what should have been given to aging parents.

Jeremiah said it well: "The heart is deceitful above all things, and desperately sick; who can understand it?" (Jer. 17:9). Apart from Jesus, we are skilled at doing all the right things for all the wrong reasons. We look like generous friends but we are driven by greed. We look like faithful friends, but only so far as something is gained. Counterfeit friendship looks selfless but underneath is selfish.

Two Houses, Two Friendships

The goal we are after as Christians is this: to move from selfish friendship to selfless friendship, from seeking our own good to seeking the good of others, from seeking to get something to seeking to give something.

But these two motivations, though extremely different at their root, can often produce the exact same fruit. For instance, one person, out of their desire to gain entrance into a popular group, may go out of their way to serve someone. While another, out of an entirely different desire to help someone struggling, may also go out of their way to serve someone. In the first case, a desire to get something was the motivation. In the second, a desire to give something. But the action that resulted was identical.

So how can we tell the difference? Jesus answers this very question in Matthew 7:24–27:

> Everyone then who hears these words of mine and does them will be like a wise man who built his house on the rock. And the rain fell, and the floods came, and the winds blew and beat on that house, but it did not fall, because it had been founded on the rock. And everyone who hears these words of mine and does not do them will be like a foolish man who built his house on the sand. And the rain fell, and the floods came, and the winds blew and beat against that house, and it fell, and great was the fall of it.

In his parable, two houses were built. From the outside they probably looked quite similar. But when the storm came a distinction emerged: one stood strong and the other collapsed. What was the difference? The foundation.

Self-centered motivations for friendship may go unnoticed for years, not causing any noticeable problems. In fact, we may perceive that our friendships are better than we ever hoped because of how they meet our needs and how easily and quickly they were built.

But what about when the storm comes? When something interferes with the friendship? What about when seasons of life change and bring new challenges? What about the inevitable problems that sin and suffering bring our way? Sometimes it is only then that the true foundation is exposed.

And, unfortunately, many friendships are built not on what Jesus taught—love God and love others—but on a worldly craving to be loved, so they collapse under the storms of life. Perhaps you've seen this happen. Maybe it's happened to you. That's what happened with Kelsey and Sarah.

When the Storm Comes

As a freshman in college, Kelsey felt uprooted and alone. Her family lived eight hours away, and most of her high school friends had chosen schools closer to home. So when she walked into the dorm room across the hall and noticed Sarah watching her favorite movie, she jumped on the opportunity. Forty minutes later, after discussing plot lines and rehearsing favorite scenes, they became fast friends.

Over time, they did everything together: studying, attending church, grocery shopping. The ease with which friendship came to them was convenient and fun. They began to see their other friends less and less. Eventually a Facebook profile picture with the label "Besties" made it official: they were best friends.

They talked and texted throughout the day, sharing their hearts and praying for one another. A day didn't feel complete for Kelsey until she had talked to Sarah. When she had a hard day, she ran to Sarah for consolation. Their friendship felt safe and provided them with stability in a relationally unstable world. It was hard for them to remember what life was like before they met.

As the school year came to a close, they made the obvious decision to live together the following semester. They already spent most of their free time together—not to mention it would save them a lot of texts and phone calls—so, in the fall, they moved into an apartment. As far as they could tell, this was a friendship as solid as they come.

But by the following summer, everything had changed. Sarah went on a mission trip and met another friend named Amy. Kelsey could tell by the Instagram updates and the lack of texts that Sarah had really connected with this new girl. She became anxious for her BFF to return. But when Sarah got home, things weren't the same. Sarah began inviting Amy into activities usually reserved for the two of them, and she often forgot about their weekly grocery trip.

The intense jealousy Kelsey felt blindsided her. She felt betrayed, hurt, and angry. She often confronted Sarah with this, but she never felt understood. Sarah always defended Amy and withdrew even more. Their once-peaceful home quickly became a war zone of arguments and tension. Kelsey was losing her best friend and didn't know how to stop it. Every attempt she made to reconcile seemed to drive the wedge further between them. What was once an unshakeable friendship was now a relationship crashing to the ground.

When the storm comes, a friendship built on sand will crumble just as quickly and easily as it was built. Every irreconcilable difference, every word of gossip, every feeling of jealousy, every hateful cold-shoulder, every resistance to healthy conflict resolution, and every refusal to forgive is rooted in the sand of self-centeredness.

Has this happened in your life? You were sure a friendship was bulletproof, as solid as they come. But then the storms of life came. One of you got married, or a parent died. A new friend disrupted your plans. Maybe he lied to you. Or she shared your secrets with another friend. Betrayal and disappointment replaced trust and enjoyment. And the house couldn't support the weight of the flood. Or maybe you weren't totally sure what happened, just that what was once a precious gift is now a dark stain on your memory.

We all tend to build our houses on the sand of our own self-centered desires. It's human nature. And the world around us knows nothing else. Self-centered friendships are so commonplace that we rarely consider them a problem. It's just how it is. But because of Jesus, there is another way. There's a better foundation for our friendships. There is hope for friendships that are lasting, stable, and life-giving. And it starts with changing our motives.

It's All About the Why

It's very difficult to spot self-love in friendship, because the activity of friendship is usually full of generosity. So the question we must learn to ask is this: *why* are we being so generous? This was the question my friend Catherine needed to ask. Catherine is a great friend! She's always eager to befriend others and is generous with her time. But occasionally, the motivation *behind* her generosity has been self-centered.

In college, she introduced two of her friends, and eventually those two friends chose to room together. She was excited for them, but also afraid of being left out. So she worked extra hard to stay close with them, often going the extra mile and missing out on other opportunities to be present with them. While this looked selfless on the outside, underneath Catherine was driven by a self-focused attempt to stay in their inner circle.

> We do not usually need transformation in our actions in friendship but in our motivation for friendship.

She told me, "I felt exhausted worrying about it all the time and often struggled with loneliness. Even when God brought my husband to me, I was scared to get married, because it might cause me to lose these girlfriends I had come to depend on."

The problem for Catherine wasn't *that* she was going the extra mile for her friends; it was *why* she was going the extra mile.

Like Catherine, we do not usually need transformation in our actions in friendship but in our motivation for friendship. This is exactly what Jesus did in his ministry: he elevated the motive above the action. It's a pattern clearly seen in his first recorded sermon, the Sermon on the Mount:

- Instead of focusing on the action of murder, he addressed the anger that motivates it. (Matt. 5:21–26)
- Instead of focusing on the action of adultery, he addressed the lust that motivates it. (Matt. 5:27–30)
- Instead of just telling the people to give, as if the action itself was enough, he told them to concern themselves with the motive of their giving. (Matt. 6:1–4)
- Instead of only telling the people to pray, as if the action itself was enough, he told them to concern themselves with the motive behind their praying. (Matt. 6:5–8)
- Instead of telling them to fast, as if the action itself was enough, he told them to be concerned with the motive of their fasting. (Matt. 6:16–18)
- And if all that wasn't clear enough, he closed his sermon with the reminder that many will come to him, hoping their good actions are enough, and he will respond that he never knew them, calling them lawbreakers. (Matt. 7:21–23)

Clearly, according to Jesus, our actions are never the primary concern. The transformation we undergo as Christians should be deeper than our activities. This doesn't mean it's okay to gossip or scream at our kids; our behavior should indeed change. But what concerns Jesus most isn't the "what"; it's the "why." If the motive is selfish, it voids the good action that follows. We see this principle clearly in his response to the Pharisees later in Matthew.

The Pharisees were the religious leaders in Jesus' day, and their teaching stood in stark contrast to his. They cared little about why you kept the law so long as you kept it, assuming right actions were God's only goal. They were the poster children for self-centered good deeds. Surprisingly, Jesus reserved his harshest words of condemnation not for the tax collectors and prostitutes but for these high-minded, law-keeping priests, pastors, and Bible-scholars:

> They do all their deeds to be seen by others. They love the place of honor at feasts and the best seats in the synagogues and greetings in the marketplaces and being called rabbi by others. They clean the outside of the cup and the plate, but inside they are full of greed and self-indulgence. They are like whitewashed tombs, which outwardly appear beautiful, but within are full of dead people's bones and all uncleanness. So they also outwardly appear righteous to others, but within are full of hypocrisy and lawlessness. You serpents, you brood of vipers, how are you to escape being sentenced to hell? (Matt. 23:5–7, 25–28, 33)

To paraphrase Jesus' words, who cares if we're praying and fasting and giving to the poor if the motives of our hearts are greed and self-indulgence? Our righteous deeds don't matter if they are birthed from an unrighteous heart. What Jesus calls for is a radical renewal of our understanding of what makes good deeds good.

How does this truth affect our friendships? By reminding us that it matters little if we swapped party friends for Bible study friends if our motivation in friendship remains unredeemed. It matters little if we're the most generous, servant-hearted, and loyal friends to others if our motivation is to be honored as that awesome Christian friend or to ensure we're never without friends ourselves. So long as we remain self-focused in friendship, like the Pharisees, our good activity is in vain.

I remember seeing the vanity of my own good deeds when I started working part-time a few years ago. The first thing I noticed in my new schedule was that I didn't have time to write letters. I know snail mail is old news to most people, but I love sending letters and small gifts to people in my life. However, with my new job, I often found I had no time for this hobby.

Often, after talking to an old friend or running into a neighbor, my first thought was, *When I get home, I'm going to send them a letter sharing a Bible verse and a small gift.* But it didn't work like that anymore. My job ate up the time I used to have, so no letters were sent.

Then an interesting thing happened: I began to feel anxious in many of my relationships. I worried about my standing with people or frequently suspected they were upset with me. Eventually God helped me see that some—not all, but some—of my motivation in writing letters was to boost my standing with others and shield myself from conflict. How could anyone be mad at me if I went the extra mile to write a note and send a gift? Surely my thoughtfulness would secure my good standing with others. Thankfully, through this change in my schedule, God began to purify my motives. It wasn't that I needed to sell my stationery and quit being generous. I needed to remove self-protection from the agenda.

When anxiety hit me because I didn't have time to write a note to a friend, I stopped to pray, for my own heart and for theirs. Praying for others was something I always had time for but, of course, wasn't something that friend would ever know about. It was the perfect solution. Simply praying for others allowed my love to be "in secret" and, therefore, not about boosting my reputation. And when I did have time to put pen to paper, I first asked God to expose and destroy any self-serving motives.

Following Jesus transforms more than simply how we do

friendship; it transforms why we do it. The entire motivation of our befriending should change as a result of our own personal metamorphosis as new creatures in Christ.

Love, the Christian's Engine

So what motive is Jesus after in friendship? What should be the new engine driving our actions?

Love.

Love for God and love for others.

Yes, it's that simple. But simple doesn't mean easy. The love Jesus calls us to is a sacrificial and sometimes painful love. In John 13:34, Jesus said, "A new commandment I give to you, that you love one another: just as I have loved you, you also are to love one another."

This is a love that does not demand its own way. A love that dies to its preferences and rights. A love that gives preference to others, even those who are our enemies. How do I know? Because in the verse above Jesus clarified that we are to love "just as he loved us." How did he love us? Through sacrifice, through taking our place on the cross.

This love is foreign to us. It is not our native tongue. Instead, we speak the language of our culture's love, which is just self-love in disguise. By default we seek out friends who will love us, not friends we can love. We walk into a room and wonder why they didn't say hi to us, not why we didn't say hi to them. We tend to ask, "What do I get out of this friendship?" and not "What can I give to this friendship?" This is natural for us. When it comes to self-love, we are fluent.

But Jesus presents a better way, a *supernatural* way: "So whatever you wish that others would do to you, do also to them, for this is the Law and the Prophets" (Matt. 7:12). Yes, the Golden Rule. (I told you it was simple.) Jesus calls us to seek the good of others, not ourselves.

Virtually no one has a problem with the Golden Rule. But while we may embrace it in theory, it's easy to exempt ourselves from applying it to our lives.

This is exactly what the lawyer did in Luke, chapter 10:

> And behold, a lawyer [an expert in religious law] stood up to put him to the test, saying, "Teacher, what shall I do to inherit eternal life?" He said to him, "What is written in the Law? How do you read it?" And he answered, "You shall love the Lord your God with all your heart and with all your soul and with all your strength and with all your mind, and your neighbor as yourself." And he said to him, "You have answered correctly; do this, and you will live." But he, desiring to justify himself, said to Jesus, "And who is my neighbor?" (v. 25–29).

Did you catch what happened? This man clearly had the right answer: love God and love others. But that didn't mean he was loving. In verses 25 and 29 we see his heart: he "stood up to put Jesus to the test" and was "seeking to justify himself." Love for others was obviously not his mode of operation. While endorsing love for God and others, he was walking in love for self.

How many of us do the same? Like referees, we act as experts on how others should love but are unwilling to get in the game ourselves. We ask the same question the lawyer did: "Who is my neighbor?" "Who exactly do I have to love this way?" We want the freedom to be selective, to decide who we will love and who we won't. But Jesus doesn't let us settle for picky love. Listen to his response to the lawyer:

> Jesus replied, "A man was going down from Jerusalem to Jericho, and he fell among robbers, who stripped him and beat him and

departed, leaving him half dead. Now by chance a priest was going down that road, and when he saw him he passed by on the other side. So likewise a Levite, when he came to the place and saw him, passed by on the other side. But a Samaritan, as he journeyed, came to where he was, and when he saw him, he had compassion. He went to him and bound up his wounds, pouring on oil and wine. Then he set him on his own animal and brought him to an inn and took care of him. And the next day he took out two denarii and gave them to the innkeeper, saying, "Take care of him, and whatever more you spend, I will repay you when I come back." *Which of these three, do you think, proved to be a neighbor to the man who fell among the robbers?*

[The lawyer] said, "The one who showed him mercy." And Jesus said to him, "You go, and do likewise." (Luke 10:30–37)

Jesus shrewdly flips the script on us and exposes the poison of our picky love. The issue is not "who is my neighbor," but "what kind of neighbor am I?" Not "who is my friend," but "what kind of friend am I?" This runs hard against the grain of our modern understanding of friendship.

Picky love is the DNA of worldly friendship. If someone is our friend, if they've done good to us and loved us, we can justify sacrificial love for them. But as soon as that friend betrays us, sins against us, or ceases to love us sacrificially, we wonder if they are really worth our time.

> The issue is not "who is my neighbor," but "what kind of neighbor am I?" Not "who is my friend," but "what kind of friend am I?"

Our picky love also shows up in another way, not just in loving those who have already done good to us, but in loving those who have the potential to benefit us in the future, showing favoritism to those who are rich in popularity, in money, or in power.

One of the college guys in our small group described this in his life: "There were a number of popular people in my ethics class last semester. When I needed a study partner or had to pick people for a group project, the decision was easy. Obviously, I would seek out the popular students, because I felt it would benefit me more to be associated with them rather than the students on the fringes." Though these students hadn't yet benefited him, they had the potential to bring him acclaim among his peers, and so he showed favoritism to them.

Jesus made it clear that this attitude is anti-Christian. He said, "If you love those who love you, what credit is that to you? Even sinners love those who love them. If you do good to those who do good to you, what credit is that to you? For even sinners do the same" (Luke 6:32–33 NASB).

It may be natural to love those who love you and do good to those who do good to you, but if you follow Christ, you are called to something more. You are called to befriend those who haven't yet befriended you, to love others who cannot benefit you. You are called to be more concerned about what kind of friend you are than what kind of friends you have. This selfless living is what Jesus' death purchased. He died so that "those who live might no longer live for themselves but for him who for their sake died and was raised" (2 Cor. 5:15).

And so now, in light of these scriptures, we can finally arrive at the Bible's stance on friendship. It's not complicated, but it's also not what we would expect. We don't find a blueprint for what our friendships should look like but rather a blueprint for what our befriending of others should look like.

We may summarize it this way: *be the kind of friend to others that you would like them to be to you.* Be a friend who loves God and loves others above yourself. This is the work we are called to in friendship.

Signs of Selfishness

Unfortunately, as we've discussed before, the giving-to-get, self-centered type of friendship is the norm. It is the model set before us by the world. It is what we grow up learning to do. It is what we see displayed in virtually every TV show, movie, and book. And that makes it much harder to spot, because it's just so . . . normal.

But does that mean it's undetectable? I don't think so. While it's difficult to detect selfishness in an isolated moment, it can be much easier to see in the patterns we cultivate over time. I've noticed three main patterns of befriending that put self in the driver's seat, three types of friends that are driven by self-love: the Demanding Friend, the Divisive Friend, and the Dependent Friend.

If you're like me, you've breathed a sigh of relief, because it's obvious you aren't *that* kind of friend to anyone. In fact, you may have already thought of several other people in your life who are these friends. But these behaviors come in much subtler ways than you might think. Let's look at each one to see how this plays out.

The Demanding Friend

Entitlement drives the demanding friend. You feel you are owed something. Even if you don't voice it, you constantly live with a sense of what your friends should be doing for you. Your list of expectations grows a mile long, and you feel justified in demanding those expectations be met. You may keep tabs in friendships, always aware of how many times you've helped them and vice versa, never forgetting the "debt of friendship" owed to you.

We may subconsciously demand that our friends never leave us, getting upset when they move away, make new friends, or simply make decisions that inhibit their time with us.

Everyone goes through hard times. Which means sometimes friendship isn't balanced. Sometimes one person is pulling all the weight and carrying their friend through a hard time. That may be a difficult season of grief, when we are doing all the listening. It may be a season of busyness, when we are doing all the initiating. It may be a season of new responsibilities, when we are doing all the supporting.

But for the demanding friend, this doesn't fly. Because when we're only in friendship to get something, being a friend to someone in need feels pointless. Why would we stay friends with someone when it only costs us something? But the Bible tells us a friend loves at all times, despite the love they get back.

In summary, you may be a demanding friend if:

- You feel entitled to receive certain things from your friends.
- You have lots of expectations, whether spoken or unspoken.
- You keep tabs with friends, always aware of who owes the other.
- You feel the right to be angry when something inhibits your friendship.
- You feel unwilling to be a friend when you're doing all the giving.

The Divisive Friend

Being divisive means fostering disunity. This can show up in many ways. The simplest, of course, is simply being a picky friend. Like the lawyer in the story earlier, we pick and choose who we extend friendship to, not based on godly character as the Proverbs encourage but based on how they can benefit us. We walk into a room and look for the cool people. We invite over for dinner the people who can help us get where we want to go. It's a way of serving ourselves in friendship that fosters cliquey communities, and for Christ followers, that's the opposite of what we want. We want communities where everyone feels welcomed and cared for.

Being divisive also means hesitating to welcome new people into the mix. New people throw off the equilibrium and threaten our position with our friends. And when our stability is found in our friendships, we form cliques and protect them.

Being divisive means we don't befriend people who we think cannot benefit us: the poor, the elderly, the outcast, and the handicapped. Or we may be unwilling to pursue friendship with people who aren't like us, people who require extra work to get to know. If friendship is all about us, then we will find the easiest route to get what we want.

Lastly, being divisive means an unwillingness to be honest. When someone hurts us, it's our job as believers to voice that. If someone is hard to be around because of their unseen sinful habits, it's our job as believers to gently speak the truth in love. But selfish friendship tempts us to avoid that awkward conversation and simply back away. Suddenly we "don't have time" to hang out, or we just stop responding to texts. Being fake and avoiding the hard conversations is self-centered and creates division in our communities.

In summary, you may be a divisive friend if:

- You pick and choose your friends based on how they can benefit you.
- You hesitate to welcome new people into your circles of friends.
- You avoid forming friendships with people who are different than you.
- You avoid the hard conversations of speaking the truth in love.
- You are a fake friend, because it's too hard to be a real one.

The Dependent Friend

Idolatry in friendship creates a dependency on our friends rather than on Christ. It causes our mood and sense of stability to vary based on how close we feel to them. When a friend becomes our idol, we begin to associate our well-being with them. Instead of holding friends open-handedly, we begin to cling tightly to them and eventually become addicted.

Addiction may sound like a strong word, but we can become addicted to anything: food, coffee, alcohol, TV, Instagram, or even people. But for those of us who have trusted in Christ, allowing for addiction is like willingly walking back into slavery. It's a waste of our freedom.

How can we know if we're addicted to something? When we cannot say no to it. The inability to say no is the definition of slavery. This is why Paul says, "You are slaves of the one whom you obey" (Rom. 6:16). For those of us who have been freed from the slavery of sin, we should not cast our freedom aside by enslaving ourselves to others. If your desire for a certain friend or friendship controls you and you cannot say no to your desire for it, it is an abuse of your freedom in Christ.

What does it look like when friendship is addictive? The most common way it shows up is constant communication. If you cannot go more than a few hours without talking, texting, or hanging out, you are likely addicted to your friend. Sometimes this shows itself in a need to share every single detail of life, as if the information you know about each other is what keeps you close. You may lose interest in every other relationship in your life, spending most of every waking moment together. Struggling to finish simple tasks like homework or housework without connecting is also common in addictive friendships.

Often our friend's approval becomes a must-have. When we sense a friend doesn't approve of us, it creates overwhelming anxiety and fear, a desperation to do whatever it takes to get it back.

When you feel addicted to someone, you become hostile toward anything that gets in the way of time with them. And when something does interfere, the experience of despair, pain, and anxiety follows close behind.

I receive a lot of emails from people sharing their friendship stories. I commonly hear people confess an intense fear of their friend starting to date or having children. The potential of a significant other or children to care for threatens to interrupt the friendship they've come to depend on. But this fear is not a sign of healthy friendship.

Lastly, an addictive friendship is often recognizable because of the extreme conflict that exists in it, a kind of break-up-and-make-up rhythm. When so much is riding on the friendship, it will inevitably heighten the emotions associated with it.

In summary, you may be a dependent friend if:

- You cannot go more than a few hours without talking, texting, or hanging out.
- You need constant communication to be okay.
- You must share every single detail of life to feel connected and close.
- You lose interest in most other relationships in your life except this one.
- You spend every possible moment together.
- You struggle to finish simple tasks like homework or housework because of this friendship.
- You associate your well-being with your ability to be close to your friend.
- You become hostile toward anything that gets in the way of the friendship.
- You feel despair, pain, or anxiety when a friend is inaccessible.
- You experience frequent and intense conflict in your friendship.

All of us, by nature, are selfish. That's the bad news. But Jesus came to set us free from living only for ourselves. That's the breathtakingly good news. Now we get to live for him, the one who died for us, and freely give love to the friends he puts in our lives. But before we get to that, we have one more mark of counterfeit friendship to cover.

Marks of a Counterfeit:
Mimicking Marriage

Our culture has given us many different examples of friendship over the years, from the backstabbing cattiness of *Mean Girls* to the devoted "urban families" of the TV shows like *Living Single* or *Friends*. In every new generation, the media has presented new models. There was Lucy and Ethel of *I Love Lucy* in the 1950s and Andy and Red from *Shawshank Redemption* in the 1990s and many more in between. But what is on the rise today is of an entirely different class. And it's most clearly seen in the language we're using.

Rebecca Traister described a friendship this way in her book *All the Single Ladies: Unmarried Women and the Rise of an Independent Nation*:

> Though [Amina and Ann's] connection wasn't sexual, the process of falling for each other was almost romantic. . . . A couple of

years after [they] began to twine their lives around each other, Ann decided to leave Washington to pursue a work opportunity. The separation was devastating.

Later in the book, Traister tells us these two friends began discussing relocation, because it was too hard on their relationship: "Amina began to make plans to leave the city. 'Ann was the center,' she said. 'And without her, there was not a lot there for me.'"[1]

Kathleen Schaefer uses similar language in her book *Text Me When You Get Home: The Evolution and Triumph of Modern Female Friendship*, released in 2018, describing friendship with words like "courtship," "friend dates," "soulmates," "life partners," and "falling in love."[2]

Schaefer, describing the friendship of one actress, writes, "At a movie screening, Michelle Williams said, 'I'm here with my best friend. I'm so in love with her. She's proof that the love of your life does not have to be a man! That's the love of my life right there.'" Another author interviewed for the book states, "What I'm talking about is how girls fall in love with their best friends. I mean, it's not a sexual thing, but . . . it was like falling in love."

Even being married doesn't seem to hinder this type of romantic language in friendship. In recounting one interview, Schaefer writes, "Stephie said to [her husband], 'Look, you know I really, really love you, but Julia is my soulmate.' 'Duh,' her husband said. 'I know.'"[3]

A New Kind of Couple

This language change is a big deal. As Albert Mohler recently noted, "Every dictator throughout history has understood a very basic lesson: if you can change the language then you can change the entire society."[4] And that's certainly true here. If your friend, not your husband, is your soulmate, there are some fairly significant implications. Which relationship will be more important to preserve when push comes to shove?

Beyond compromising our loyalty in marriage, there are other significant changes. Is it any wonder that using language traditionally saved for romantic (sexual) relationships would blur the lines physically in friendships?

Both Schaefer's and Traister's books, as well as the study I cited in chapter 1 from the *Journal of Men and Masculinities*, mention increased physical affection as part of this shift in friendships. One participant in the men's study said, "I think most guys in bromances cuddle . . . It's not a sexual thing, either. It shows you care."[5]

The increase in intensity and physicality in friendship is also seen in the popular Instagram hashtag #ibfhug (read: Internet Best Friend Hug). These are friends, often very young, who have met and become close online. And when they finally find a way to "break the distance" and meet in person, they film their meeting. In almost every video you'll witness two friends running toward each other, embracing like lovers, and falling on the ground crying and cuddling.

Social media is clearly helping popularize these new expressions of friendship, but others are turning to film and television to reflect this newfound friend-love.

Schaefer writes:

> We're reappropriating our friends as our people and soulmates. We're writing movies and television shows that take the way we are together seriously. We're tilting our culture by insisting on a solid spot for ourselves and our friendships in it, and a wider audience is responding.[6]

Echoing this sentiment, Traister cites one television show:

> Writer, director, and actress Lena Dunham has called female friendship "the true romance" of her show, *Girls*. And, indeed, the

opening scene of its premiere episode showed Dunham's heroine, Hannah Horvath, waking up in bed, spooning her best friend, Marnie, who has taken refuge with Hannah both in an effort to escape being touched by her boyfriend, and because the two women wanted to stay up late watching Mary Tyler Moore reruns.[7]

Here's the point: this is a form of friendship that mimics marriage. Sure, it might not technically be sexual, but many of the characteristics of a marriage are present: exclusivity, romance, physical closeness, and promise-making. These kinds of "covenants" may express themselves in permanent matching tattoos, in actual best-friend contracts, or in phrases like this one: "Best friends: it's not just a label, it's a promise."[8]

The magazine *Marie Claire* describes this new friendship trend in an article entitled "Are Girlfriends the New Husbands?":

> Across the nation, tens of thousands of single women are in committed quasi-unions with their closest confidantes, behaving like married couples in virtually every respect (save for the sex, of course). They hit up family functions together, stand in as emergency contacts on doctors' forms, even cosign mortgages together. In other words, if your mother's been nudging you to settle down and find a husband already, tell her to relax, you've kind of, sort of, got one.[9]

And in case you thought this was just a trend relegated to women, listen to *Psychology Today* describe the latest trend in male friendship:

> A bromance, to the men in the study, was similar to a romance with a woman, except for the lack of any desire for sex. The participants said things like, "We are basically like a couple," and "They are like a guy girlfriend." These bromances usually included: disclosure of personal matters, sharing secrets with the bromantic partner and no

one else, overt expressions of emotions, feelings of trust and love, willingness to be vulnerable, and hugging, kissing, and cuddling—all regarded as non-sexual. (All but one of the men said that they had cuddled with a bromantic partner. All 30 said that their physical interactions were not about sexual desire.)[10]

Should a Friend Be "Your Person"?

The fictional friendship on the show *Grey's Anatomy* between characters Meredith and Cristina changed the landscape of friendship. It's these two that coined the now-popular phrase, "You're my person."

What does it mean for someone to be your person? According to several sources and its use in the show, "a person isn't only your best friend, they're more; your 'person' is your everything."[11]

And there are plenty of people on the hunt for their person—not in marriage, mind you, but in friendship. Bumble, traditionally a digital dating app, now offers a friendship version: Bumble BFF. It's one of several new friend-finder apps where you'll spot profiles sporting things like, "Looking for the Meredith to my Cristina."

So is it okay for a friend to be more than a friend? Is it right for a friend to be your person? Let me answer with a clear *no*.

The Bible is clear that marriage is the only relationship to be exclusive and binding. No other human relationship gets the title of "one flesh." No other human relationship has "you-belong-to-me" ownership. No other human relationship calls for lifelong commitment (Gen. 2:24; 1 Cor. 7:4, 39). While there is one example of two friends making a covenant (David and Jonathan), the context and purpose of that covenant is vastly different than that of marriage. It is not a prescriptive blueprint for friendship but rather a descriptive example of a kingdom-centered friendship in very rare circumstances. (For more on this, see appendix 1.)

It is certainly good to have friends who stick closer than a brother. But it is not good to have friends with whom we are one flesh. Treating a friendship with the weight, exclusivity, and ownership of a marriage is unbiblical and inappropriate. It undermines the institution of marriage and all that marriage points to: the union of Christ and the Church (Eph. 5:31–33).

This is a serious allegation. The institution of marriage has been created by God and for God and exists to showcase truths about God. Forming friendships that mimic and usurp this holy institution is to directly defy God's good design for marriage and compromise the glorious truths it is meant to show.

This also puts future marriage covenants at risk. Can you see the predicament? If you've already created a covenantal union with your BFF, how can you enter into one with a spouse? This is why some maid-of-honor speeches sound like the groom is butting his way into something sacred. Or why a popular new pose in wedding photography has emerged where the best friend and bride have their hands intertwined behind the groom's back. Google it. It's real. Both cases reveal that exclusive friendships are in competition with newly formed marriages.

> Treating a friendship with the weight, exclusivity, and ownership of a marriage is unbiblical and inappropriate.

Just to be clear, this kind of friendship can pose a threat to marriage *after* you are married as well. When unresolved hurts exist in a marriage, it can be tempting to look to a best friend for what you lack with your spouse.

Recently, my friend Annika was faced with this very situation. She met a new friend at church, a wife and mom in her mid-thirties. They hit it off immediately, but Annika quickly began to feel uneasy about it. Her new friend was having marriage problems and constantly spoke negatively of her husband, often saying she'd rather open up to a friend than to him.

Annika did her best to be a good friend, but it never seemed to be enough. If she wasn't available or if she spent time with other friends, she was met with comments like, "You're clearly too busy for me," or "If you cared about me, you would be here when I needed you." Over time it became apparent to Annika that this woman was turning to friendship for the closeness and intimacy she was lacking in her marriage. Instead of doing the hard work of pursuing reconciliation in her marriage, she pursued friendship. Thankfully, Annika knew this wasn't the kind of healthy friendship she needed and wisely took a step back from the situation. She brought other friends and church members into the mix who could provide support and lovingly confront this dissatisfied wife. Though it was extremely difficult for her, Annika refused to allow their friendship to replace her friend's marriage.

Whether we are single or married, forming friendships that mimic or undermine marriage is wrong. They hinder the formation and endurance of healthy marriages that are meant to point to Jesus, and they keep us looking to our friends to quench the thirst in our souls.

Let's remember what we learned in chapter 1: friendship truly is a great thing worth pursuing, but it cannot satisfy our deepest longings. It is a treasureless field. The pursuit of this golden calf of human love may find expression in both romantic relationships and in friendships. But in both instances, if it is a substitute for Christ as our fountain of living water, it is sinful.

Marriage Is Also a Treasureless Field

So why do we face this temptation in friendship? First, because exclusivity makes us feel safe. It insulates us from rejection (or so we think) and seems to guarantee a loneliness-free existence. It creates at least one place where we always belong. Let's be honest, the idea that someone would promise to be there for us no matter what is attractive. This is why so many are drawn to marriage. Which leads to my next point.

The temptation to create marriage-mimicking friendships exists, because we are convinced that marriage itself will satisfy and complete us. Undoubtedly, marriage is a treasured gift many Christians will receive. Instituted by God before the Fall, and intended to showcase the beauty of the gospel, marriage ought to be highly regarded by God's people. But marriage is no savior. It cannot rescue, redeem, or ultimately fulfill us. It has no final power to save us from our loneliness, emptiness, or purposelessness. Believing marriage can do the work of God himself is serving an idol. Marriage, like friendship, is a treasureless field.

Nonetheless, many continue to believe that marriage can satisfy. And so the inability to achieve married status can then lead to despair. And as hopes of engagement fade, many singles settle for what seems to be second best, an exclusive friendship: *Finally, I found someone who gets me, the one with whom I belong: my best friend.*

Sadly, there is a whole new movement within Christianity that would say there's nothing wrong with this. In fact, they are fighting for the legitimization of vowed or covenanted friendship, specifically for those who struggle with same-sex attraction.[12]

Wesley Hill, author of *Spiritual Friendship*, said it this way:

> If marriage offers husband and wife the opportunity to cultivate long-term fidelity and the quiet intimacy of a shared history . . . then I need a way of being single that affords me a similar (though not identical) opportunity. . . . Recovering the historic Christian practice of vowed friendships can help with all of these needs.[13]

Hill, in an article on his website, proposes covenanted friendship as a solution for gay couples who want to adhere to a biblical sexual ethic. Evidently, "not sleeping together didn't mean they needed to stop living together or considering their relationship as a 'forsaking all others' sort of commitment." Hill states, "It seems to me, 'vowed' or 'covenanted' friendship might be *precisely* the right pastoral model for such a couple."[14]

While this seems to provide the companionship many single people long for, it is not a biblical solution. It is a counterfeit friendship that keeps us from looking to Christ as the solution to all our longings.

Yes, we need friends. We need community. But never in a way that imitates marriage. Does that mean that some won't experience the exclusive intimacy that marriage offers? Yes. But marriage is not where fullness of joy is found anyway. It cannot and will not fully satisfy the human heart's desire for connection. It is only the shadow; union with Christ is the substance. Only union with Christ can quench the thirsty soul.

Signs of Mimicking Marriage

How can we spot a friendship that might be mimicking marriage? There are five main symptoms usually present: exclusivity, jealousy, romantic language, craving physical connection, and a lack of boundaries.

Before we get into them, please note that there can be other causes for these symptoms. Sometimes people use romantic language in friendships because that's all the world has modeled or because they have never considered it being inappropriate in friendship. Sometimes an exclusive, just-us-two friendship exists because of circumstances like serving together as missionaries in a foreign country. And some people are just more physically affectionate than others. None of those examples are necessarily signs of an unhealthy friendship. But when most or all of these symptoms are present in a friendship, we should be concerned.

Exclusivity

Exclusivity happens when two friends begin to wall themselves off from others and refuse to let others into their friendship. Sometimes this happens through the use of language and labels, such as "we're each other's best friends" or "you wouldn't understand" (that is, you're on the outside). Sometimes it's through activities, like constantly arranging hangouts that no one else is ever invited to and doesn't know about. Other times it's through secret sharing. If your BFF is the *only one* who knows these things about you, it creates a kind of exclusive bond, a way to secure their presence in your life.

Jealousy

Jealousy is directly linked to ownership. In marriage, a husband belongs to his wife and vice versa (1 Cor. 7:4). There is a healthy possessiveness that should exist in a marriage.

I'm not talking about *envy*. Envy is wanting something that someone else has. But *jealousy* is an intolerance of rivals. I will not tolerate any woman who attempts to gain my husband's romantic affections. Why? Because Jimmy is *my husband*, and no one else's. Jealousy is an intolerance of all that rivals what is rightly yours.

But we never own our friends; they do not belong to us. So when we feel jealousy for a friend, it is a red flag. Jealousy is becoming frustrated when someone else is hanging out with our friend. It is becoming angry at new relationships she or he might be forming, either with other friends or with a potential spouse. Sometimes it isn't other people but activities that become the rival to our friendship, things like ministries, sports, or hobbies that threaten to take away what we feel is rightfully ours: time alone with our friend.

Romantic Language

Romantic language is common in exclusive relationships like marriage. So it's no surprise that an exclusive friendship may reveal itself in language. This is usually only a problem in female friendships, because it is more culturally acceptable. But the growing use of the term "bromance" shows it has surfaced in male friendships as well.

Examples of romantic language include affirmations of physical attractiveness ("You're so hot." "I love your body."), proclamations of love ("I love you endlessly." "You're my soulmate." "You're my other half."), declarations of ownership ("That's my girl." "She's my BFF, you can't have her."), and statements of neediness ("If I ever lost you, I would lose myself." "You don't realize how much I need you.").

Lack of Boundaries

A lack of boundaries is common when two friends are acting as one. In marriage, many lines (not all) are removed: we join houses, bank accounts, and names. So when a friendship begins to erase boundary lines, when it becomes difficult to discern where one ends and the other begins, it is unhealthy.

It's normal for there to be friends who have more access to you than others. In my life, there are a handful of people with whom I've cultivated trust and camaraderie over many years of friendship. We have given each other deeper access into our lives. These are the people who walk in my back door unannounced, who help themselves to food in the pantry, who invite themselves over and shamelessly ask for favors.

But even in my dearest friendships we maintain a kind of separateness, a respectful understanding that we are individual women who must answer to God and be loyal first to him. While we have, when necessary, shared beds when we travel together and changed in the same room, we maintain a measure of modesty around each other, knowing that our bodies belong to God and our spouses.

Erasing all boundaries and all modesty in the name of best friendship is no longer friendship meant to cultivate intimacy with God, but friendship meant to cultivate intimacy with each other.

Craving Physical Connection

Craving physical connection is different than *being* physically affectionate. Physical touch is a good thing. It's great to give hugs to our friends, to walk arm in arm, to hold hands while praying, or to rub someone's back in moments of grief. Touch is a good and needed thing in a friendship. But, when we foster exclusivity in a friendship, touch can cease to be an expression of our love and instead become something we need to feel connected. When we begin to crave physical closeness with someone for physical closeness's sake, it is a red flag.

How can you tell if this is a problem? When you need to be constantly touching your friend, when you regularly cuddle together, frequently give each other back rubs, or feel the need to hide your physical closeness from others, it should alert you that something is off.

In healthy friendships, the goal of physical affection is to express care for the other person. It is not required but given freely. In unhealthy friendships, the goal of physical affection is to satisfy your own desires for closeness and care. It becomes necessary and is often demanded.

Same-Sex Attraction in Friendship

This is a good time to address an aspect of this topic that, for many, is a sensitive one. Same-sex attraction is a complex issue, and while this is *not* a book about same-sex attraction, it is a common enough issue in this setting of marriage-mimicking friendships that I would be remiss not to mention it here.

Worshipping created things (friendships) can and does result in warped sexual desires (Rom. 1:24–27). It is not uncommon for the prolonged idolatry of a friend (I cannot live without him/her) to eventually awaken the temptation to act out sexually with them. In fact, a major reason I began writing about friendship in the first place is because so many of my friends found themselves in this very predicament. They had never experienced same-sex attraction before and were often so focused on their own longing for a husband that they would have laughed at the thought of ever sinning sexually with a friend.

But as they mindlessly formed and enjoyed marriage-like friendships, sexual desires began to creep in. My friends were both surprised and deeply alarmed at how right and natural these desires felt. As I walked alongside them and tried to help them pick up the pieces, it was apparent that the same-sex attraction or homosexual behavior was the fruit of the deeper problem: they had made their friend an idol.

The same has been true for many more who write me emails and share their own stories of unhealthy friendships. This makes this an unavoidable issue for me, because not mentioning it wouldn't serve people as well as I feel I should.

Thankfully, the Bible brings such clarity on this matter. Romans 1 plainly shows us that disordered loves (love for friend above love for God) leads to disordered desires. We experience confusion because our world is shouting a different message, one that absolves us from all culpability. And while the world's solution may give some explanation for our symptoms, it doesn't address the true source of the problem.

For someone who experiences sexual desires for a friend, the world says, "You're just bisexual, and you didn't know it." But the Bible says, "You are just a sinner in need of a savior." The world attaches the heavy burden of identity to our sexual desires and tells us to figure it out. But the Bible points out the root of the problem—sin—and provides the solution—Christ.

> Disordered loves lead to disordered desires.

I know the issue of same-sex attraction is far more complex than what I've just addressed here. Idolatry of friends is certainly not the only thing that awakens same-sex attraction. I only mean to present it as *one* possible catalyst. If you want to read more about this, check out appendix 2 for a more thorough discussion and some additional resources.

In summary, a friendship is mimicking marriage when:

- It is exclusive and isolated.
- You feel jealous and possessive of your friend.
- You fear your friend getting married or growing closer to their spouse.
- You are hesitant to make plans that don't include your friend.
- You feel free to "speak for" your friend.
- You have begun to tie your finances together.
- You begin to use romantic or sensual language toward each other.
- You have frequent sleepovers and often share beds.
- You crave physical connection to each other.
- You have a "no-boundaries" culture where nothing is off-limits.

Good Gardeners Pull Weeds

A true gardener understands that just because something flourishes in the soil does not mean it's good. Weeds often grow faster and easier than healthy plants. A true lover of flowers will learn to identify weeds, so they can pull them out at first sight. But pulling weeds—removing things that are growing—is not a sign that you hate plants. Rather, it's a sign that you love them.

I love friendship and long for it to grow and flourish in my life and in yours. Because I love it, it's my desire to draw friendships out of the dark of isolation and secrecy, to give them the living water of friendship with God, and to pull out the weeds of sin that choke them out.

These chapters are my attempt to describe what friendship weeds look like. This is necessary because, in my experience, many people cannot tell a weed from a flower in friendship, so those weeds of sin grow fast and choke out any real flower that has started to grow. But the goal is not to make you afraid of friendship or hesitant to cultivate deep and meaningful relationships with others. Quite the opposite! I hope it will build your confidence in how to create and sustain solid, stable, and satisfying friendships with Christ as the rock-solid foundation.

Maybe after reading the last few chapters you're feeling discouraged. Maybe you never thought you had a problem with friendship until today. Maybe you've known a certain friendship in your life is unhealthy, and now you can no longer ignore it.

Wherever you find yourself, don't be discouraged. We all experience the temptation to look to friendship for more than it can give. It is a temptation that Jesus himself has experienced and has been victorious over (Heb. 4:15)! He is a capable and compassionate savior to all who turn to him. No situation, however complicated it may seem, is too much for him.

But please, don't foolishly ignore the warning signs. Avoiding our problems may preserve surface-level peace for now, but it will make them harder to handle later. Not only that, avoiding our problems is a sign we don't actually love our friendships. People who love their gardens notice the weeds and pull them quickly. People who love their friendships will do the same.

So where does change begin? Well, how do you pull a weed? You grab it from the root. That means we cannot start with changing our friendships or changing our circumstances, though those things may need to change. We start at the root of the problem: we have sinned against God by how we've misused and idolized friendship. And, therefore, we start with repentance.

God Problems

It was my fourth year at summer camp with our youth group in Panama City, Florida, and quickly proving to be the least enjoyable. My best friends at the church had all graduated, and most of the students my age had formed close-knit groups that I didn't fit into. Who were my people? For the first time in my life, I didn't know.

As we were dismissed from the morning service into our two hours of free time, I began to wonder, who would be my friend? Who would reach out? Who would invite me into their plans?

As God would have it, the answer was . . . no one. I walked awkwardly around the camp grounds trying not to look as pitiful as I felt. Wandering onto the beach, I saw people I knew. They nodded and smiled as they continued to chat with their friends. I kept waiting for an invitation that never came.

This confirmed what I had already felt about my youth group: it was super cliquey and exclusive. On Sundays the center of the youth room was visibly segmented into groups by school and popularity, while the edges were dotted by isolated individuals who sat alone. This bothered me so deeply that I had previously asked my parents if I could attend a different church.

Obviously, nothing had changed. The solution, therefore, was to somehow show all those self-centered people the error of their ways or simply find a new, less-cliquey group of people to be friends with. Neither option seemed feasible that afternoon, so I decided to go for a walk on the beach and complain to God.

I spent the first twenty minutes of prayer detailing the self-centered attitudes of all my peers, how they refused to think about anyone other than themselves. After exhausting my list of grievances, I did something dangerous: I asked God to speak to me. I let my mind rest from rehearsing the actions of the inconsiderate people in my youth group and began to notice the waves and the beauty of the Floridian coast.

Suddenly, a passage of Scripture I had read that morning came to mind:

> Who shut in the sea with doors
>   when it burst out from the womb,
> when I made clouds its garment
>   and thick darkness its swaddling band,
> and prescribed limits for it
>   and set bars and doors, and said
> "Thus far shall you come, and no farther,
>   and here shall your proud waves be stayed"?
> (Job 38:8–11)

The sand beneath my feet became sacred ground as I walked the line my God set for the waves. I gave myself over to contemplating his awesome power. *How great is my God that he exercises this much sovereignty over our earth? And somehow, he cares for me?!* Slowly, my lack of companionship faded away in the face of the abundance in front of me. *The One who tells the waves where to stop is my friend!*

After pondering this, a few things became apparent: I saw that I had refused to see God as my all in all. Though I had his attention and affection, it wasn't enough for me. I preferred the attention of my peers, which had made me entirely self-centered. Despite my complaints of their lack of concern for me, I realized I didn't really care about them myself. I wanted something *from* them, not something *for* them.

With genuine grief in my heart, I asked God to forgive my self-centered thinking and rejection of him. I finally saw the root of my issue clearly: I had forsaken him, the fountain of living water, and had sought out the broken cistern of friendship.

I returned to the beach with my circumstances undisturbed. All my peers were still disinterested in me, but to my surprise, something had shifted in me. I found myself beginning to approach *them*. I started up conversations with *them*. I asked *them* questions. I became interested in *them*. I began to care about *their* lives, *their* days, and what *they* had learned in our first teaching session that morning.

You see, I was the one who needed a transformation. In restoring God to his proper place I was finally able to care about someone other than myself. My self-obsession had morphed into self-forgetfulness. My desperate need for someone to notice me had turned into a happy desire to notice others. I finally felt liberated to freely love those God had put around me.

And by God's grace this transformation wasn't temporary. After camp was over, I saw Sundays differently too. Instead of seeing a room of inconsiderate people, I saw opportunities to be a friend to others.

What we're after in this book is sturdy friendship. Friendship that can withstand the storms of life. We want friendships that reflect the kingdom we're a part of, a kingdom of people who sacrificially love one another the way Jesus sacrificially loved us. But to get that, we must start in the right place: recognizing that our problems in friendship aren't really people problems, they're God problems.

The Essence of Sin

We tend to evaluate sin based on how bad it looks on the outside or how harmful it is to others. If it looks nice and isn't hurting anyone, it's probably fine. But this way of thinking betrays our poor understanding of the essence of sin.

When we consider the activity of Adam and Eve's sin in Genesis 3, it doesn't seem that heinous a crime. Not something we would likely see on the evening news. They ate a piece of fruit. So what? What's so dangerous about that? And yet, Romans 5 tells us this first sin brought about condemnation and death for all people. So what does this tell us about the nature of sin?

One thing is clear: sin isn't primarily about the action. God had encouraged them to eat the fruit of any of the other trees in the garden. If eating fruit from a tree isn't necessarily sinful, what made the eating from one specific tree sinful? Simply this: God had told them not to. Underneath their eating was a distrust and rejection of God.

The essence of that first sin—and all sin since—is a turning away from God. In the book of Hosea, God describes this first sin as the breaking of a covenant: "But like Adam they transgressed the covenant; there they dealt faithlessly with me" (Hos. 6:7). Paul uses the language of devotion in 2 Corinthians 11:3: "But I am afraid that as the serpent deceived Eve by his cunning, your thoughts will be led astray from a sincere and pure devotion to Christ."

Covenant-breaking. Faithlessness. Devotion-forsaking. These are the words the Bible uses to describe the eating of a piece of fruit. We see here that sin is not so much about what we do but rather Who we leave. At the heart of sin is a proclamation: God is not enough. Sin is not primarily an issue of wrong deeds but wrong loves.

In fact, God often likens himself as a spouse: "For your Maker is your husband, the Lord of hosts is his name; and the Holy One of Israel is your Redeemer, the God of the whole earth he is called. For the Lord has called you like a wife deserted and grieved in spirit, like a wife of youth when she is cast off, says your God" (Isa. 54:5–6).

So if God is a husband to us, then our rejection of him is like adultery. This adultery is the theme of the book of Hosea, appearing this way in God's opening words: "for the land commits great whoredom by forsaking the LORD" (Hos. 1:2). This word "forsake" literally means they ceased following God. It wasn't so much an aggressive rejection of God as it was an apathetic abandoning of him as their first love. And, consequently, that apathy opened the door for them to pursue other loves and make other things their priority. Our God is a personal God, and so our sin is personal to him, as personal as a wife committing adultery on her faithful husband.

> Sin is not primarily an issue of wrong deeds but wrong loves.

You see, idolatry is easy to see when the objects of our affections are immoral (illegal drugs or illicit sex), but much harder to see when what we worship are God's good gifts. It's often the very best things in life that cause the greatest threat to our loyalty to God. Husbands, wives, children, friends, jobs, ministries: these are all great things! But when they receive our highest affections and become the center of gravity in our lives, it is a grievous offense to God. It matters little what we prefer above God, only that we prefer it to him.

Repentance: The Only Remedy

If the root of our sin is a rejection of God, then the solution is very simple: return to him. This act of turning to God and away from our sin is called repentance. It's the recognition that we cannot fix our wayward hearts, that we are not able to heal ourselves. We can only go to the healer of our souls and ask him to restore us. Change in our friendships starts with repentance, with putting God back on the throne in our lives.

Listen to my friend Megan describe this process of repentance in her own life:

I needed my friends to need me, want me, admire me, care for me, and spend time with me. I craved their love so badly. Their words and actions affected me more than anything, so I bounced between the extremes of deep happiness when they gave me the attention I wanted and deep pain and angst when they didn't.

I knew I needed God, but I was blinded by the depths of idolatry I was in. I refused to believe that he could fulfill every need I had, that he was my portion. My heart longed to be made much of, and I was seeking that in the attention, affection, and approval of my friends.

Then, I moved overseas for five months to serve a few missionary families. After being away for a while, I finally realized what the Lord had done: he had literally put me on a mountain on the other side of the world without friends. He purposefully picked me up and set me far away from the things that my heart was clinging to.

I realized I had made my friendships an idol, and I cared way more deeply about their relationships with me than I did about my relationship with the Lord. I also realized, in making my life revolve around my friends, I was actually trying to make it revolve around me.

It was during this wilderness season that I learned life wasn't about me and it wasn't about my friends. It was about the Lord. I needed him to survive this world of brokenness. As he moved me away from caring primarily about myself and others, I began to crave him more. I longed for time in the Word, time in prayer with him, time thinking on what he was doing in the world around me.

This miracle was something only the Holy Spirit could have performed in my heart! Over five months, there was a huge shift in how I saw the world. It wasn't about me; it was about Jesus and his glory. There was no room left for me, and that meant my friendships needed to become ways to glorify him, not myself.[1]

In repentance we agree with God that idolizing friends is sinful and worthy of punishment. In repentance we receive Jesus' life, death, and resurrection as sufficient to restore us to right standing with God. In repentance we recognize that we cannot fix our sin; we cannot treat it ourselves. Repentance is going to the healer of our souls and asking him to restore what we cannot. Change in our friendships starts with repentance, with returning to the fountain of living waters and drinking deeply.

But isn't repentance to be avoided? Isn't the admission of sin a sign of failure? Maybe to the world, but not for the Christian. In 1 John we're reminded that the greater failure is to act as if we have no sin:

> If we say we have no sin, we deceive ourselves, and the truth is not in us. If we confess our sins, he is faithful and just to forgive us our sins and to cleanse us from all unrighteousness. If we say we have not sinned, we make him a liar, and his word is not in us. (1 John 1:8–10)

Be encouraged, friend. If you are beginning to see sinful tendencies in your friendships, that is a gracious invitation from God to confess and return to him, the only one who can restore you. Don't avoid this very necessary and normal part of the Christian life. And know that you are not alone. The problem of sin and idolatry in friendship—in all its variations and intensities—is common. Join the rest of us by daily returning to God when you wander away and trusting in Jesus' righteousness, not your own.

Repentance Means Restitution

Returning to God by confessing our sin is where repentance begins. But it isn't where it ends. True repentance will overflow into our relationships with others.

This is clearly seen in Zacchaeus's conversion in Luke 19. A despised tax collector who had become rich by defrauding his fellow Jews, Zacchaeus responded to Jesus' kindness with not just a change of heart but a change of behavior:

> And Zacchaeus stood and said to the Lord, "Behold, Lord, the half of my goods I give to the poor. And if I have defrauded anyone of anything, I restore it fourfold." And Jesus said to him, "Today salvation has come to this house, since he also is a son of Abraham." (Luke 19:8–9)

Our sin is always first and foremost against God (Ps. 51:4). But if our sin has affected others in our lives, then repentance means we need to work to right those wrongs, if possible. This is called restitution. Let's briefly look at what restitution will look like for each of our friendship counterfeits we observed in chapters 2 through 4.

If we have allowed a friend to replace Jesus in our lives, most of our restitution will be directed toward the Lord. It is Jesus we have sidelined, and so it is Jesus we need to make amends to. There may not even be a need to bring anything up to a friend besides apologizing for putting so much pressure on them.

If we have been selfish in our friendships, our need for restitution is likely a little higher. At a minimum, it means confessing our sin to our friends and asking for their forgiveness. We may need to

True repentance will overflow into our relationships with others.

approach those closest to us and share that we now recognize a pattern to be demanding or divisive or dependent, and to apologize for how that has affected them. We may even ask our friends to help us by speaking up when we fall into those habits again.

If we have allowed our friendships to mimic marriage, our need for restitution is the highest, because, in this case, restitution means changing the very nature of a friendship. It means working to undo the ways it has become marriage-like. I'd highly recommend getting other godly men or women to be involved in this process. Go to a mentor, a pastor, or another godly friend, and let them know you have a friendship that isn't healthy and need their help to move it in a right direction.

Though God is always after unity and reconciliation in our relationships with others, there are definitely times when repentance means ending a friendship, at least temporarily. For example, if you've been sexually immoral with your friend, then separation is crucial. If you're wondering if it's time to end a friendship, see appendix 3 for some help in this.

Sometimes Repentance Is a Wilderness

Be forewarned, leaning into repentance doesn't immediately change how we feel. Our feelings of anxiety when someone isn't available or debilitating fear when a friend is about to move may linger. Often it takes a season of God retraining our hearts and minds to experience the freedom that is already ours. This season of cultivating dependency on God can feel like a wilderness, a difficult season of sanctification.

For Megan, it meant a literal wilderness. She spent five months overseas without one friend. But by stripping her of all friendships, God taught her to depend on him. She learned that Jesus is enough

when he was all she had. In that isolated season, she learned to cultivate friendship with God. And when she came home, everything was
different.

Sadly, many people equate the barren, lonely, stripped-down season of the wilderness with evidence that God doesn't love them. But
nothing could be further from the truth.

In the Bible, God often sends those he loves to the wilderness. In
Hosea 2:14, God says of his people: "Therefore, behold, I will allure
her, and bring her into the *wilderness*, and speak tenderly to her." In
Deuteronomy 8:14–16, God reminds his chosen people of their forty
years in the wilderness:

> Take care lest you forget . . . the LORD your God, who brought you
> out of the land of Egypt, out of the house of slavery, who *led you*
> through the great and terrifying *wilderness*, with its fiery serpents
> and scorpions and thirsty ground where there was no water, who
> *brought you water* out of the flinty rock, who *fed you* in the *wil-
> derness* with manna that your fathers did not know, that he might
> humble you and test you, *to do you good in the end.*

What was God up to those forty years the Israelites spent in the
wilderness? He was leading them, feeding them, and humbling them
so that they would recognize that he was their provider. God was trying to cultivate their dependency on him, not on people. He is often
up to the same things in us: leading us, sustaining us, and helping us
see it's God we really need.

The Saving Friendship

My walk on the beach during that summer youth camp was a moment of communion with God that quenched a deep thirst in my soul. It enabled me to build a foundation for friendship that didn't center on myself. The living water of knowing Jesus gave me the power to live for someone other than myself. Instead of looking for what I could get, I began looking for what I could give. Friendship with God saved my friendships with others.

Like any relationship, it has its ups and downs. Some days God feels so near I could touch him and others not so much. But overall, I'm seeing the daily pursuit of God produce consistent fruit in my friendships.

Now that God is my stability, I can hold my friends with open hands. If they move or change jobs, if they get married or have children, it's okay. I can love them and support them through the changes, because my daily friendship with God is what I'm clinging to for stability.

Now that God is my closest companion, I am less threatened by new friends and my own seasons of transition. Even in the moment when nobody is available to be there, I have a companion in God himself who carries me through.

Now that being God's friend is my significance, I am free from comparison and competition in my friendships. I can be interested in anyone, not just the "important" people, because the most important person in the universe has already said, "I want to be your friend."

I'm sure this all sounds good theoretically, but I know many people do not know God this way, such that he actually feels like a true companion, a real person in their life who matters to them. Please hear me: if that doesn't change, if our knowledge of God is only theoretical and not actual, our flesh-and-blood friends will always look more appealing.

My hope in this chapter is to carve a clear path to cultivating friendship with God and to help you understand the reasons we often avoid drawing near to him.

First Things First

In Matthew 22:36–40, Jesus is asked a question:

> "Teacher, which is the great commandment in the Law?" And [Jesus] said to him, "You shall love the Lord your God with all your heart and with all your soul and with all your mind. This is the great and first commandment. And a second is like it: You shall love your neighbor as yourself. On these two commandments depend all the Law and the Prophets."

Jesus gives two commands: love God with all that you are and love your neighbor as yourself. But the order matters here. The greatest and most urgent thing is always to love God. But this isn't how most of us think. When we have problems in our friendships, our first thought usually isn't to work on our relationship with God. We have a people problem, not a God-problem, right? *I love God, and I know he loves me. We're good. It's my friends (or lack thereof) whom I have a problem with.*

If you are refusing to cultivate this all-encompassing love for God until you have friends who love you well, you've got it backward. We will not be able to work out this friendship thing until we give sufficient attention to our relationship with God.

This commandment reversal came up a lot when I interviewed people for this book. Many voiced a belief that they could not or would not pursue God seriously until they had a solid community of people around them to do this with. Good community, it seemed to them, was the gatekeeper to fellowship with God. But the Bible says there is only one gatekeeper between God and man, and that's not our community, it's Jesus (1 Tim. 2:5). When I suggested that they should start seeking God first, with or without good community in place, it was a foreign thought.

But we have another bad habit. Not only do we reverse the order of the commands, we make it about getting love, not giving love.

We rewrite the command to read, "I need to know God loves me with all that he is. I need to know others love me." But God says, "You need to love me with all that you are. You need to love others as yourself."

According to Jesus, what we need to do most is *not* to seek to be loved but to seek to give love. Did you catch that? The two great commands are *not* (1) make sure you meditate on how much God loves you and (2) find others to love you. Contrary to popular belief, our souls are the healthiest when they aren't seeking love but giving love, first to God and second to others.

That's why we must start building the house of friendships with a foundation of loving God. If we do not learn how to love him, we will have no hope to love others well. Love for God is the power source; love for others is the output.

Timothy is a perfect example of this. In Philippians 2, Paul writes about him to the church at Philippi. See if you can catch the connection he makes between love for God and love for others: "For I have no one like [Timothy], who will be genuinely concerned for your welfare. For they all seek their own interests, not those of Jesus Christ" (Phil 2:20–21).

Timothy was genuinely concerned for the welfare of others. He loved people well, like we hope to. But why was Timothy so loving? The answer is in the next verse: he did not seek his own interest but the interest of Jesus Christ.

Now if I had to guess how that last sentence ended, I would have said, "For they all seek their own interests, not the interests of *others*." But it doesn't say that. The opposite of seeking your own interests is seeking the interests of Jesus. What enabled Timothy to love others well? It's the same thing that will enable us: being first and foremost concerned with Jesus.

> Love for God is the power source; love for others is the output.

Maybe you've never been able to cultivate the meaningful friendships you've hoped for. Maybe you thought you had a healthy friendship, but it turned out to be full of idolatry. According to the text, the problem might be that you aren't very interested in Jesus. Our first step in cultivating healthy friendships with people is cultivating a friendship with God.

I know you might be eager at this point to skip ahead and see what friendship should look like in your day-to-day life or to learn how to be a good friend, how to deal with conflict, and other practical issues. But we cannot start there. We mustn't start there. This chapter is the foundation and, by far, the most important truth to get in this whole book. Because without cultivating friendship with God, we have no hope of rightly befriending one another.

God Is Not Math

Recently Jimmy had a conversation with a mentor, Phil, where he shared a fear of not using every opportunity God had given him for ministry. He really wanted to do the best job he could with all the pressing opportunities. Surprisingly, Phil's simple answer was this: "Jimmy, God's not math." Implication: loving God is not an equation. It's not about doing things for God and *poof!* you get results; it's about knowing him.

Sadly, many people relate to God as if he is a math equation, not a person. We input our good deeds (X) and our religious activity (Y), and we expect it to equal him blessing us with a prosperous life and good relationships (Z). We may not say it out loud, but our actions say it for us.

When we treat God like math, we care only to know what is expected of us. *Tell me what to do to keep God happy, so he will give me what I want.* We're glad to do what he wants us to do, so long as he holds up his end of the deal. But Christianity is about knowing, not doing.

We see this clearly in Jesus' words in Matthew 7:21–23:

Not everyone who says to me, "Lord, Lord," will enter the kingdom of heaven, but the one who does the will of my Father who is in heaven. On that day many will say to me, "Lord, Lord, did we not prophesy in your name, and cast out demons in your name, and do many mighty works in your name?" And then will I declare to them, "*I never knew you*; depart from me, you workers of lawlessness."

It mattered little how much these people did for Jesus; what mattered was whether or not they *knew* him. The same concept shows up in Jeremiah 9:23–24:

> Thus says the LORD: "Let not the wise man boast in his wisdom, let not the mighty man boast in his might, let not the rich man boast in his riches, but let him who boasts boast in this, *that he understands and knows me,* that I am the LORD who practices steadfast love, justice, and righteousness in the earth. For in these things I delight, declares the LORD."

God desires people who will brag about the fact that they know him, not that they have done great things for him. The idea of knowing God is a frequent theme in the book of Hosea. In chapter five, verse four, God accuses his people of spiritual adultery against him with these words: "For the spirit of whoredom is within them, and *they know not the* LORD." And then he clarifies what he desires from them. It is not a list of good works to do, but simply to love and know God: "For I desire *steadfast love* and not sacrifice, *the knowledge of God* rather than burnt offerings" (Hos. 6:6).

God is not only after our external obedience; he is after our hearts. He is looking for hearts that desire and delight in him above all else. This is what it means to have eternal life: to know and love God through Jesus his son (John 17:3).

The Cost of Knowing God

Before we spend any time looking at how we are to get to know God, a public service announcement is in order. If you are serious about pursuing him, it will cost you. Jesus knew this. As often as he said things like "I am the bread of life," (John 6:35), he also said, "Whoever does not bear his own cross and come after me cannot be my disciple" (Luke 14:27). It is expensive to know Jesus.

What exactly will it cost us to take seriously this charge to love God with all that we are? To cultivate friendship with him? The fee is three things: exposure, patience, and faith.

Exposure

Buyer beware: friendship with God is not as warm and fuzzy as some would have you think. Drawing near to God is different than drawing near to anyone else. Unlike our friends, God is perfect. Holy. Sinless. Glorious. High and lifted up. As we draw near to him, it will, by nature, expose how far from perfect we find ourselves. Intimacy with God requires a revelation of our own depravity.

This pattern is seen in several moments in the Bible. Isaiah gets a close-up view of God, high, exalted, and seated on the throne, and his first words are "Woe is me. I am a man of unclean lips." Drawing near to God exposed his sinful nature. When Peter first encounters Jesus in the miracle catch of fish, he responds to Jesus with "Get away from me. I am a sinful man." Over and over again we see the pattern: draw near to God, become aware of your utter sinfulness apart from him.

Drawing near to God shines a light on the dark corners of our hearts, exposing our secret self-obsession. It removes the rose-colored glasses and forces us to see the truth that apart from him we have no good.

Friendship with God will cost you your pride. And for many, that price is too steep. So keeping God at arms' length while committing to do good Christian deeds seems like a fine alternative. *Who will notice anyway?* But doing for God is not the same as loving God. To love him we must draw near to admire his character, and when we do, we will be forced to own the selfishness in us.

But please remember, this is not bad news! We do not become more sinful by approaching God; we simply become aware of the sinfulness that was already there. This awareness only deepens our love for the work of Jesus. It causes us to cling more tightly to him and loosens our grip on our own works. Nothing could be safer for our souls.

Patience

The biggest pushback I get when I encourage people that God can satisfy their relational longings is this: *but God can't talk back to me.* It's true, when you call up a friend and share your thoughts, they respond instantly. When you share your grief with a friend, they put their arm around you. Not so with God. He is unseen and intangible, at least right now. But he is just as real and just as responsive. Over and over again the Bible tell us the Lord speaks. He responds. He interacts. He sees. He pays attention.

But there's a catch. We must wait for him.

Cultivating friendship with God requires patience. It requires delayed gratification. And in our instant, fast-paced world, it is a high price. Interacting with God is more like writing letters back and forth than talking on the phone. When we pursue him by reading his word and praying, we write a letter. Several days of this may pass while we wait anxiously for the arrival of a response. And when it comes, like a personal letter in the mailbox, we soak it up and respond back.

God's responses come most often as we read his word, but they may also come in the form of a sermon on a Sunday morning, the encouragement of a friend, or by his Spirit reminding us of truths we already know in the quietness of our hearts. Once it came to me in the form of a journal.

Years ago, I had a big decision to make about a job and was seeking God about it. But I felt as though my prayers were bouncing off the ceiling. As each day passed and the time for decision-making drew near, I grew weary in waiting and prayed, "Are you going to answer me, Father? Will you show me which way to go?" Later that same day, I was given a journal with this verse on the front: "Call to me and I will answer you, and will tell you great and hidden things that you have not known" (Jer. 33:3). Though he eventually made it clear which way to go, on that day I had all I really wanted: the assurance that God was real, that he was my Father, and that I could count on him to lead me. This assurance didn't come right away but after many days of earnest prayer and a stubborn determination to hear a response.

The spiritual discipline of waiting on God is both active and hopeful. It is a determined, focused effort of expectation. A stubborn refusal to move on until he responds to our pleas. The good news is God has promised many things to those who wait on him: they will never be ashamed (Ps. 25:3), they will not grow tired or weary (Isa. 40:31), they will be heard and responded to (Ps. 40:1), and God will act on their behalf (Isa. 64:4). It is a cost worth embracing.

Faith

In a way, friendship with God is a long-distance relationship. While we are here on earth, we are away from the Lord. Yes, God is with us through his Spirit in us, but still, we cannot see him face to face. And isn't that what we all long for? But in this life, it is not an option. And so, for now, knowing God means we must know him by faith, not by sight.

For many, this is the reason they refrain from pursuing God. It seems unfathomable that an unseen God can be known in a meaningful way. Chasing down friendships with other people looks far easier and more satisfying. But, while it may be easier, it is not more satisfying. Only knowing Jesus by faith will fill the hungry soul.

Thankfully, this long-distance thing is only temporary! Like a couple enduring the almost-but-not-yet season of engagement, we endure because we know the wedding feast is coming. One day, we will be united physically with the God we love. One day, we will get to speak with him face-to-face and feel the warmth of his embrace.

But for now, we eagerly study his Word and believe what it says about him. By faith, we pray and believe that he hears us. By faith, we wait for his response. And though it isn't ideal to be apart from the One our soul loves, knowing him in this life is still a joy far superior to all others.

Making the Intangible Tangible

Building a friendship with God requires exposure, patience, and faith. Though it might seem costly, this is the call of every Christian. It is our greatest commandment, our primary objective, our daily goal to love God with all our hearts, souls, minds, and strength; therefore the cost is worth it. There is no other foundation than this. Building our life on anything else will eventually fail us.

Once we've counted the cost, we have questions: How do we know a God we cannot see? How do we depend on a friendship with a God we cannot sit across from?

It's imperative that we talk about this in very frank terms. Too often our discussion in this area is so impractical and cloaked in Christianese that, when we are left alone in our room trying to draw near to God, we have no idea what to do. Let's change that.

There are doubtless many ways a Christian can grow nearer to God: singing worship songs, spending time in nature, and listening to sermons, just to name a few. But there are three that rise above the rest, just as there are some diamonds that shine with more brilliance than others. The three primary ways God has given us to draw near to him are reading our Bibles, praying, and being a part of a local church. Before you shout "duh" at your book and move on to the next chapter, hear me out. This is not only about learning how to do these things, but understanding why they matter in relationship to God. Knowing why you are doing something is half the battle.

The Word

All relationships are built on information. When I first began dating my husband, our dates consisted mainly of information-sharing: what our favorite books were, where we went to school, what we were studying, a history of our lives up to that point, what we liked and didn't like. All of that information helped us build a framework for the other person's personality and character. Slowly over time, we began to deeply love the character we saw in one another. Our love began with facts.

The Bible gives us information about God. What he likes, what he doesn't like, a history of his activity in the world up until now, his favorite places and people, what he makes a habit of doing or not doing, his responses to other people's activity, what makes him angry and what makes him rejoice. If we read our Bibles to learn information about God, it will help us build a framework for the character of God. And slowly over time, you may find that you deeply love the character you see.

> The Bible is not primarily a book about us and what we should do; it is a book about God and what he has done.

Remember, the Bible is not primarily a book about us and what we should do; it is a book about God and what he has done. Therefore, read it to learn more about God above all other objectives.

A simple way to apply this is by reading through each book of the Bible and keeping a list of all the things you learn about God as you go. It may be new things; it may be things you already knew. Learning facts about God is the first step to loving God. As Jen Wilkin said, "The heart cannot love what the mind does not know."[1] It is true of human relationships, and it is true of our relationship with God.

Prayer

We cannot stop with simply reading the Bible and learning information about God. In John 5:39–40 Jesus rebukes the Bible scholars of his day, saying, "You search the Scriptures because you think that in them you have eternal life; and it is they that bear witness about me, *yet you refuse to come to me* that you may have life."

Knowing things *about* God is not enough. You can be an expert on him and still not know him personally. So how do we know him personally? As Jesus said in the verses above, we must *go to him*. We do this through praying. Praying is simply talking to God. We take what we learn in the Bible about God and then talk to him about it in prayer.

When we read about his compassion for sinners like us, we come in prayer, thanking him for showing us compassion. When we read that he hates the proud, we come to him in prayer and confess our pride, asking for his help to rid us of it. When we read that Jesus is the only righteous one, we come to him in prayer and ask for faith to trust his good deeds and not our own. When we read things we don't understand, we come to him in prayer and ask him questions and for help to understand.

If we have only Bible reading and no prayer, we are not becoming friends of God, but students only. Like following a stranger on social media, we may know a lot about them, but we do not really know them. Yes, we must study God's character, but if we refuse to take the next step of praying, we are no different than the unbelieving Pharisees. We must read the Bible relationally, always talking to the One who wrote it.

Everyone's prayer life will look different. But I can confidently say that only praying while you are going about your day is not enough. How do I know? Because that is not enough to build a meaningful friendship with anyone. The relationships we care most dearly about are the ones we schedule extended time for. We need set-apart time for prayer the same way we set time aside for anyone we want to know better.

So what can this time of prayer look like? It might be writing our prayers in a journal at the kitchen table. It might be praying on our knees in the closet, reminding ourselves of how desperately we need God's help. We might read the psalms out loud, letting the words of saints who've gone before us be the script when we're unsure of what to say. We may stand with outstretched hands in a moment of longing to be with him. Or if we don't have time to be alone, it might be praying on our knees on the kitchen rug while the kids run laps around us. Whatever you do, finding time to talk to God is necessary if we hope to intimately know him.

Lastly, we must be listeners in prayer. Have you ever had a friend who did all the talking and rarely listened or asked you questions? Not a very deep friendship, was it? No relationship can thrive when it's only one way. While Bible reading is the primary way we listen to God, giving five to ten minutes of silence in our prayer times is helpful. It allows our minds to calm down and provides space for the still, small voice of the Spirit to remind us of what we've read in his Word and to prick our memory of any unconfessed sin.

When I sit quietly with God, I often simply stare out my window at the trees in my backyard and think on all I just learned about God in his Word. Those quiet moments allow me to meditate on the reality of God—that he created this world that I see around me—and to respond to anything he lays on my heart.

Do you have a daily time to meet alone with God? I'd encourage you to decide today when and where you will meet with him and what book of the Bible you'll begin to study. All the nearness with God I experience in my life is rooted in this simple, daily habit.

The Local Church

Cultivating intimacy with God begins when we're alone but doesn't stop there. Remember, following Jesus is an individual decision, but it is not an individual assignment. We cannot and should not do this journey alone. I'm assuming you're already convinced of this, because you're reading a book about friendship. But cultivating Christian friendships alone is not enough. We need the community provided by a local church.

Churches provide a safe place for the family of God to do life together. They provide structure and authority, giving protection to the vulnerable. They, like our extended families, are full of people of all ages providing spiritual mentors for many. They allow singles to be set in families and widows to be cared for.

The local church is a nonnegotiable in our relationship with God. Since we have been adopted by God into his family, we now have brothers and sisters in the faith. And while it might feel safer to pick and choose which Christians we want to do life with outside of any congregation, this is not God's design for us.

We need the ministry of the local church in our lives. We need other believers to walk with us and help us see when we are walking blindly in sin. We need other believers to physically help us when we are suffering or too weak to run to God. We need other believers to speak the truth to us when we are struggling to believe it.

God has often made himself tangible to me through my local church. In some of my darkest hours, it was members of my church who gathered around me and who lifted me up in prayer. When I needed direction, the pastors and elders of my church were there to provide guidance. These other believers are often the literal hands and feet of Jesus to us.

Sure, our local churches have problems. They are full of fellow sinners like us. But drawing near to God requires us to draw near to his other children. So if you haven't yet, find a church near you that preaches and practices the gospel of Jesus, that upholds and teaches the whole of the Bible, and become a member.

Living Water, Our Only Hope

Knowing God changes everything. It is what we were made for. And when we begin to do what we were made for, we thrive. Friendship with God saves us. It sets us on solid ground. It is the foundation that holds the walls in place on the stormiest day and the darkest night. Laying a foundation is hard and unseen work. But nothing could be more important in our pursuit of stable friendships than this.

Though God is unseen to our eyes, meaningful friendship with him is possible. If you will count the cost and seriously pursue him in the word, in prayer, and in a local church, I believe you'll find yourself resonating with Peter's words in 1 Peter 1:8–9:

> Though you have not seen him, you love him. Though you do not now see him, you believe in him and *rejoice with joy that is inexpressible and filled with glory*, obtaining the outcome of your faith, the salvation of your souls.

When all our deepest needs are met in Jesus, we no longer enter the field of friendship starving for affection. Rather, we come to friendship with a spring of water overflowing from our hearts. Then, when the world creates television shows where "the love affair at the heart of the show" is between two friends who are "comedically codependent," we can say, "No, ultimate dependency on anyone but God is idolatry, and my friends challenge me to lean on him alone." When we hear the world say, "Romantic relationships are fleeting, but friendships are *everything*," we can say, "No, Jesus is everything, and my friends help me see that."

Only drinking the living water of friendship with Christ enables us to reject the lies the world is selling and to be the kind of friends we are called to be.

7

Ripping Up Roofs

Redefining Friendship

Imagine you grew up in a remote village without clean water. Everyone you know suffers from some form of ailment because of the contaminated water, but it's just a part of life there. This is how it's always been.

What does it mean to be a good friend in this situation? When someone runs out of water, you share the extra you have that day. If someone experiences the familiar symptoms of parasites, you listen and empathize because you've been there.

But one day, a man you've never seen before crosses your path. He tells you—unbelievable as it may sound—that there is a freshwater spring just minutes away, a short walk through the forest, in the one area your village avoids because supposedly it's haunted.

You decide to risk it and, sure enough, just where he said, you find a pool of water sourced by a bubbling freshwater spring. Not only does the water look and smell different, it actually tastes good. Rather than reminding you of your thirst like the water you're used to, this water actually satisfies.

Running back to your village, you herald the good news of this discovery. You convince as many people as possible to risk a walk through the so-called haunted woods and follow you to the source of freshwater.

Though not everyone will follow, this new discovery has forever redefined what you need, and what everyone else needs. Being satisfied at the freshwater spring changes your perspective on what it means to be a friend. No longer does friendship look like offering a glass of contaminated water from your home. No longer does it mean hopelessly empathizing with the pain of various illnesses. Now, being a real friend means getting others to that life-giving freshwater spring.

Redefining Friendship

One taste of living water changes everything. Formerly accustomed to continual thirst, we now experience lasting joy. Our souls, once hollow and lifeless, are now full of life and vitality. But eating living bread and drinking living water doesn't just change us; it changes how we do friendship. Specifically, it redefines:

1. What it means to befriend
2. Who we befriend
3. How we befriend

We cannot look at another soul, someone in as much need of Jesus as we are, and not do all we can to bring them to the source of life and joy. For anyone who has tasted and seen that the Lord is good, love for others will always ask: how can I help them get more of Jesus in their lives?

This is exactly what we see the four friends in Mark 2:3–5 doing:

And they came, bringing to him a paralytic carried by four men. And when they could not get near him because of the crowd, they removed the roof above him, and when they had made an opening, they let down the bed on which the paralytic lay. And when Jesus saw their faith, he said to the paralytic, "Son, your sins are forgiven."

We don't know who initiated this desperate rooftop entrance. For all we know, the paralytic may have been too hopeless to try to see Jesus. Or maybe he didn't think it would do any good. But regardless of how the man on the mat felt, we at least know his friends were convinced it was worth the effort. Their faith in Jesus shaped their understanding of what being a good friend meant.

The culture around us hasn't found the freshwater spring yet. It hasn't tasted and seen the goodness of the Lord, so it will define true friendship in different terms. To the world, friendship itself is the highest joy friendship offers. So the goal becomes drinking up as much joy as possible from one another. But we know that trying to get lasting joy from another human is like drinking salt water—it will only deepen our thirst. Though worldly friendship means well, it cannot provide what it is selling.

> Eating living bread and drinking living water doesn't just change us; it changes how we do friendship.

But unlike the world, we've discovered the freshwater spring and know, as Paul did, that compared to knowing Jesus everything else is rubbish (Phil. 3:8). The greatest good we can do for our friends is the same thing the four friends did for the paralytic: whatever it takes to get them closer to Christ, even if it means tearing up a roof.

Redefining What It Means to Befriend

Likely you won't ever face a situation where ripping the roof off a building is the right way to apply this principle. So what does it look like for us to be this kind of friend to others?

At a very basic level it means *pointing any unbelieving friends to Christ*. To those still drinking foul water, the most loving thing we can do is to point them to the freshwater spring. We are ambassadors for Christ, imploring our friends that Jesus is where eternal life is found. Of course, that doesn't mean every conversation includes a gospel presentation, otherwise you won't have that friend for long! But it at least means you long for their highest good and look for every opportunity to point to Jesus in both word and deed.

One of my closest friends through junior high and high school was a devout Muslim. Shaheen and I grew up together. We ate at one another's houses, knew each other's families, and weathered difficult storms together, like 9-11 (a very terrifying time for Muslim families) and the traumatic death of our mutual friend's mother.

But when issues of religion came up, I either downplayed or avoided the truth that I believed with all my heart: that Jesus alone is our hope for eternal life. I assumed being a good friend meant avoiding the gospel so as not to offend her.

Finally, in college, out of deep love for her, I spoke honestly about Jesus. I told her that God is so good and holy that no one can get to him through good works alone, including the five pillars her faith was founded on. Rather, I told her, Jesus is the only person who can get us to God because he alone obeyed perfectly and lived a sinless life, because he's God. And he died in our place, atoning for our failures. It is only in him that a way to God has been secured for us.

Well, as you may have guessed, this conversation made things fairly awkward in our friendship. By pointing to Christ I had inserted a level of tension and conflict to our friendship. And since I was so afraid of conflict at the time, I slowly backed away from our friendship. I justified this by assuming she would no longer want to be my friend anyway.

But nothing could have been further from the truth. Later, Shaheen wrote me a letter sharing how hurt she was. Surprisingly, she wasn't hurt by *what* I shared. She knew I was a Christian and already knew what I believed. She was hurt that I didn't continue in friendship despite the tension. While I'm so glad I was finally honest about my faith, I deeply regret not leaning into this tension and fighting for friendship with Shaheen.

If we hope to have close friendships with those who don't know Jesus—and we should hope for this—we must be willing to welcome this tension. It's important to be honest and upfront about our faith. Avoiding what is most important to us to preserve surface-level peace is a form of fake friendship. But we also must be willing to welcome the tension this honesty brings. Please learn from my mistakes: don't avoid the truth and then drop it like a bomb and run away. Instead, be honest from day one about what Jesus means to you and then don't back away. Ask good questions about what your friends believe and why and listen well. Seek to understand their point of view and be interested in their life. Yes, we should be willing to lovingly challenge others, but we should also be faithful and trustworthy friends, not just to those who believe like us but to those who do not.

So, being a roof-ripping friend means first pointing our friends to Jesus and welcoming the tension. Secondly, it means *properly dealing with your own neediness.*

One day in the fall of 2015, I arrived at my empty home feeling lonely. Jimmy was out on tour, and I was playing the role of single mom again. As my heart quickly filled with self-pity, I brainstormed which friend I should call. Subconsciously, I knew I needed to pray, but I felt distant from God and didn't feel like talking to him. Plus, I knew my present state of self-centeredness would quickly be confronted in prayer, and I wanted to indulge my woe-is-me attitude a little longer. Maybe a friend would listen to my current tale of woe and comfort me with her sympathy.

I knew the barriers that choice laid between me and my savior. I knew I was avoiding the repentance my soul needed, effectually starving myself by refusing to drink the living water Jesus offers. But I didn't want to agree with God about my selfishness.

And so I made several calls and sent several texts, but to no avail. Why were none of my friends responding? Alone in my bedroom, I felt pretty needy. I just *needed* someone to talk to. I *needed* someone to love me. I *needed* someone to comfort me.

We all face moments of neediness, those feelings of overwhelming desperation for friendship. And being a good friend means properly addressing this neediness. It means recognizing Jesus as the greatest good we need.

It was a good thing none of my friends responded, because I could no longer avoid the inevitable. I knelt down to pray. It quickly became apparent that this was truly what I needed. I needed to let God pull the weed of entitlement wedging itself in my soul, and when I did, like every time before, this living water quickly swallowed up my needs and quenched my thirst.

Properly addressing our neediness may mean being slower to reach out to our friends when what we really need is to pray. Using our friends to avoid Jesus is a misuse of friendship. When we're feeling needy, it's worth asking: Is my soul right with the Lord? Am I reaching out because I don't believe Jesus is enough for me? Am I searching for affirmation that is already mine in Christ?

Lastly, being a roof-ripping friend means *properly dealing with the neediness of others*. I had a friend in high school who gradually became possessive of me. She began to call all the time and wanted to do whatever I did. I preferred to float around the cafeteria at lunchtime visiting with different people, but she requested I sit next to her every day. Eventually, her words began to betray her heart: she felt like she needed me to thrive and even felt closer to God around me. She had associated her well-being with me.

There are two ways we usually respond to clinginess like this. We either run away as fast as we can because we're uncomfortable, or we embrace the savior role we're being given because we like feeling needed. But neither response is right, because neither points the other person to Jesus.

With my friend in high school, I chose to run. It was too much pressure and I was afraid of disappointing her, so avoiding her seemed like the best solution. But that resulted in a much greater conflict. Eventually we had a heart-to-heart, and I was able to tell her that all the good things she saw in my life were directly sourced from the stream of Jesus, my fountain of living waters. I told her I wanted to be her friend but could not do so in the way she wanted me to, and I encouraged her to seek God for herself.

When we encounter the neediness of others in friendship, we must resist the urge to run away or to rescue. Our job in these moments is to point to Christ, to take our friend by the hand to the only place her needs can be met.

Redefining Who We Befriend

Getting a taste of living water doesn't just affect how we define good friendship; it also affects who we choose to befriend. Because all our needs are met in Christ, we can now be a friend to all.

Don't misread that. I didn't say be friends *with* all. We're limited people, and we cannot have hundreds of friends (sorry, Facebook). But we should be friends *to* all. This means we are not picky in our befriending. We extend friendship to whomever God has placed around us, not just those we click with. Remember, the second command is to love your *neighbor* as yourself. If you're wondering who to befriend, start by looking at who God has already placed nearby. These are quite literally the neighbors, the nearby people, you are called to love.

We need to stop for a moment and address a common myth: great friendship is based on compatibility. Yes, there are some people we have an easier time getting along with. And there's nothing wrong with that! These are the people who have similar personalities to us, with similar preferences and common interests. Building friendships with people who are like us is easy, because it doesn't cost us much to love them. But while it is not wrong to have compatible friends, it is not an indicator of anything special.

Rather, it is the people with whom our personalities and preferences clash the most that force us to exhibit the truest form of love—a sacrificial love. To befriend people who aren't like us requires that we set aside our own desires and tendencies to extend friendship to them. This is what Jesus calls us to: extending friendship not just to people we click with but to those who rub us the wrong way.

Being a friend to all also means befriending those who don't seem to offer us anything in return. Children, adults with special needs, the elderly, the unpopular, and the poor are a few examples.

If we only befriend those who can obviously give something back to us, aren't we only giving to get? Aren't we simply befriending others out of love for ourselves? Choose to pursue friendships with people who don't enhance your social circle and can't pad your bank account. If you do, I promise you'll be rewarded with a different kind of wealth. Because the kingdom of God belongs to the poor in spirit.

There was a girl who often sat alone at our church's youth services. One day, I sat next to her and introduced myself. Her name was Carmela. Though she was about my age, it became apparent as we talked that cognitively she was much younger. I'm not sure what kind of mental disability Carmela had, but I quickly saw why she didn't have friends.

As the year went on, I frequently sat with her. And soon, a friendship blossomed between us. I will never forget the day she remembered my birthday and gave me a thoughtful card. I was shocked at her generous heart. Here she was, frequently ignored by her peers and yet exhibiting kindness, not bitterness.

Carmela taught me so much about what true friendship is. She set the bar high for me, being kind to others when very few had been kind to her. Of course, there were times when I longed to insert myself into the circles of popular kids nearby. Who doesn't want to be popular and important? But then I would see Carmela and her shining example of contentment and kindness. At the end of the day, I decided I wanted to be more like her.

Jesus' command was not to love your Christian neighbor as yourself, but simply to love your neighbor.

Lastly, being a friend to all means extending friendship outside the walls of our churches. Yes, it is imperative we have community with those who share our faith—this is why local church membership is a nonnegotiable for Christians. But Jesus' command was not to love your *Christian* neighbor as yourself, but simply to love your neighbor. We must be willing to extend friendship to neighbors, family members, coworkers, and others who do not share our faith, not because they are projects to be fixed but because they are people to be loved. Because our souls are satisfied in the fountain of Christ, not in one another, we are free to extend friendship to whomever God puts around us, no matter what they believe.

Redefining How We Befriend

Being satisfied by the living water of friendship with God redefines what it means to befriend and who we befriend. But practically, how do we do this? In the daily grind of friendship, how does friendship with God change our patterns and behaviors? To say it simplistically, it makes us friends who are in it to give. Friends who are more interested in wanting something *for* others than wanting something *from* them. Knowing God should make us generous to others, not greedy. Let's look at how this generosity should manifest.

1. Because Jesus is our stability, we can be open-handed.

When you are in friendship to give, you hold friends with open hands. Though this is one of the most challenging aspects of selfless friendship, it's one of the most important. Because at the end of the day, we have no right to demand commitments from other individuals. While local churches do provide a committed community for us to be a part of (more on this in the next chapter), as friends, inside or outside the church, we are individuals who answer to God.

Therefore, Christian friendship calls us to cultivate deep and meaningful relationships without individual obligations. This is the scariest part of friendship for most people. For many, it feels safer to wait until someone has committed to us before we share our hearts. But, as we've talked about, the Bible gives us no space to create commitment or obligations in this arena. This is why Jesus must be our stability. It is our friendship with him that enables us to cultivate depth with others while remaining open-handed.

I have several really close friends who have recently moved away. We used to live five minutes away from each other, and now two of those women are on the other side of the Dallas-Fort Worth area (read: one hour away) and one is now twenty-five minutes away. Their respective moves have had a huge impact on the way we enjoy our friendships. The time and frequency with which we meet has been drastically reduced, something I've often grieved. But I have no right to demand that they continue to be present in my life in the same way they did when we all lived in the same town. I must hold them with open hands by allowing them the space to be obedient to God and to cultivate new friendships locally.

This happens all the time as friends of ours make familial transitions, get married, and have children and grandchildren. With each new season there are new responsibilities. And so with each new season there are new limitations and priorities. Our job in friendship is to be givers, seeking to fight for our friends' obedience to God in these priorities, not take away from them by demanding they meet our needs.

The most Christ-like thing my friends have ever done for me is encourage me to obey God in new seasons by being flexible in what our friendship looks like due to the new responsibilities God gives me. They are only able to do this because their worth does not come from our friendship, but from Christ.

Our friends do not answer to us; they answer to God. He is their king, their Lord, their first loyalty. It is not right to put ourselves above God in others' lives. If, in God's purposes and sovereignty, he changes their season of life, their availability, their responsibilities, it is our role as a friend to encourage and support that, even if it means a loss for us. This is the sacrificial love we are called to in friendship.

Being open-handed also means we allow our friends to have other friends. We do not own them; they do not own us. They do not belong to us. So when and if new relationships crop up in their lives, we can celebrate that, not grieve it. And when seeing our good friends cultivate new friendships produces insecurity in us, we run to Jesus and take another drink of living water so that we can continue coming to the arena of friendship with a spirit of giving, not taking.

If being this open-handed in your friendships feels terrifying, it may be a sign that friends have too high a place in your life. When our souls are well fed at the fountain of living water, we can continue extending friendship through the ebb and flow of these life changes.

But being open-handed doesn't mean being unemotional. The loss of a good thing is always worth grieving, and friendship is a really good thing. When a friend moves away, tears rightly reflect the value of that friendship. When new responsibilities in our lives limit our connectedness in certain friendships, sorrow is normal and good. Good friends grieve to be separated. As David wept to leave Jonathan, so we should grieve the losses we experience in friendship, but those losses should not undo us. Healthy friendship grieves with open hands, allowing and encouraging our friends to go where God leads. It's when we tighten our grip and demand our friends stay near us that we can know our grief is not flowing from a good place.

2. Because Jesus is our companion, we can be interested.

Rick Warren famously said, "True humility is not thinking less of yourself; it is thinking of yourself less."[1] Because Jesus is our friend, we no longer walk into a room alone and in need of friendship. He is with us! We are liberated to be a companion to someone else, rather than seeking one out for ourselves. We are free to be the most interested person in the room, not the most interesting. Because the God of the universe has miraculously shown interest in sinners such as us, we can have our eyes open to what's happening with others.

You don't have to be an extroverted, life-of-the-party type of person to apply this. It simply means that you are willing to greet others rather than waiting to be greeted. It means choosing to ask about their lives rather than looking for ways to share about yours. Good friends initiate conversations, ask questions, and listen well.

Being interested in others also means not focusing all your efforts on just one friend or one group of friends. It's tempting to refuse to make new friends once you've got your tribe all set. But a soul that is satisfied in Christ is a soul that can be interested in new people, even when they have solid friendships. Because their main source of companionship is coming from Jesus, not from earthly relationships.

3. Because Jesus is our significance, we can be unoffended and self-controlled.

We all know what it feels like to be left out. To see that picture on social media of a party we weren't invited to. To see the wedding invitation we never got on someone else's refrigerator. To not get asked to be on the worship team at church. So how does friendship with Jesus affect this unavoidable and often uncomfortable part of life? Our friendship with Jesus reminds us that we already have more honor and significance than any human inner circle can provide us with.

If we boil it down, being included is about being honored. Like the kids picked first for the kickball team, being chosen for any group or gathering is a position of honor. It's our pride that is offended, the pride of wanting to be important in human circles.

But when we choose to find our significance in Jesus, it frees us to be unoffended when we are left out. Though human honor often looks more attractive than the honor God gives, we can resist temptation by reminding ourselves of the truth. We remember our high standing as sons and daughters of God. We remind our hearts that the highest honor and privilege anyone could ever have is already ours: being called "friend" by the maker of the universe! Believing these things releases us to take rejection on earth in stride, remembering our job is to be a generous friend to others, not a bitter one.

Being unoffended also enables us to see situations from others' points of view, knowing that birthday parties, weddings, and gatherings cost money and no one can afford to invite everyone. It enables us to be considerate and content.

But can I be honest with you for a minute? I haven't mastered this friendship thing. It's often still challenging to do well. Don't fool yourself that because I wrote a book about it that I never struggle with these issues. Walking these things out is hard!

You see, fighting for joy in Jesus is a daily decision, not a one-time-fix. Like the newly freed Israelites in the wilderness, we, too, need to collect manna every single day to keep our souls fed in Christ. Once a week is not enough. And sometimes I grow lax in my daily manna collection, setting aside my relationship with God for one reason or another. It's in those times that the temptation to look to friendship for satisfaction is strongest. But part of being a good friend to others means resisting this temptation by exhibiting self-control.

Like me, you too will probably find this to be a daily battle. The temptation to trust in friends instead of Christ will pop up frequently. But knowing that our significance is found in Jesus means we don't have to give in to temptation. We can be self-controlled by running to Jesus in those moments of insecurity rather than our friends.

When we feel unstable about our friendships and our place in them, instead of sending cryptic leading texts ("I know you're probably too busy for me today . . .") or fighting tooth and nail for one-on-one time with a certain friend, we can make time to read the Word and talk to God in prayer. And then pray for our friends and seek their good, not just our own.

Exercising self-control in friendship has another application: self-censorship. Now what do I mean by that? Isn't it good to be fully known and bring everything into the light? Yes. One hundred percent yes. We are commanded to confess our sins to one another and not let sins dwell in the darkness. So by all means, let us be people who share the darkest corners of our hearts with a handful of trusted friends who will preach the gospel to us and continually point us to Jesus.

But there is a form of sharing that is actually a selfish attempt to create intimacy and obligations. It is a form of sharing not to give something or grow closer to Jesus but to gain something from a friend. In some cases, it can be an unhealthy form of marriage-mimicking, where the desire is to know 100 percent of someone else and have them know 100 percent of you. This type of sharing is birthed from a thirsty soul.

But we know the only intimacy that truly satisfies is intimacy with

God. The best and healthiest intimacy in friendship cannot satisfy the soul. Even the best and healthiest intimacy in marriage cannot satisfy the soul. Only knowing God through Jesus satisfies. Only Christ offers living water.

So what does godly self-censorship look like? It means choosing *not* to share every single thought you had and feeling you felt that day. Choosing *not* to demand to know every single detail about someone's life and story. This keeps our friendships ingrown, focused on one another and not on Jesus and his kingdom.

Before you give in to the need to share it all or find it all out, ask yourself: Why am I sharing? Is it to fill a need to be known, heard, loved, and seen? Am I struggling to believe that God knowing, hearing, loving, and seeing me is enough? Am I operating out of a thirst only God can satisfy? Or out of love for others?

Just to clarify, I know a lot about my closest friends. I know how they met Jesus; I know the painful sins others have committed against them and the ones they've inflicted on others. I know the unbelief they battle and the lies they struggle to resist. I know their tendencies and preferences. And they know these things about me too. It is not wrong to know and share these things. But this knowledge did not come overnight. There is no such thing as instant intimacy. True love and trust in a friendship come over years of running side by side toward Jesus, sharing those details as they pertain to our current battles of faith.

But, let me be clear, my friendships with these women are not made secure because of the information we know about one another. Our friendship is secure because we are fighting to reach the same finish line: to stay faithful to Jesus until we take our last breaths. Our friendship is secure because we share a common goal to be devoted to Jesus above all else. The information we know about each other is a side effect of our friendship, not the foundation of it.

Ultimately, this desire to have someone know all of us is met in

God. What a comfort that he says he knows us better than we know ourselves. He alone knows the depths of our hearts, when we sit up and lie down. He knows the words we are going to say before we say them. He sees us and loves us in ways no one else can (Ps. 139). And we should not try to reproduce this type of omniscient (all-knowing) love apart from him. We don't need our friends to know every little detail, because God already does and his love is enough. Because Jesus is our significance, we can be self-controlled.

Knowing Jesus produces such freedom in friendship! It brings joy and delight into our social circles as we extend kindness to a lost and dying world by being the friend to others that Jesus has been to us. Let's work hard for these Christ-centered, joy-filled, and freeing friendships. Friendships that find their source of joy in Jesus. Friendships so great that the watching world begins to wonder how they can get in on it too.

But is good friendship only about giving? Sure, Jesus meets all our needs, but aren't there also things we need from earthly friendships? Let's talk about that next.

Not Good to Be Alone

Redefining Our Needs

Without a doubt, some of you have had a question growing as you've worked through these chapters. If God is our stability and Jesus our closest companion, and if friendship with him is our source of significance and he is supposed to be "our everything," then is it the case that we just don't need anything from our friends?

Of course not!

When God said, "It is not good that the man should be alone," he wasn't only referring to marriage (Gen. 2:18). There are no lone rangers in God's kingdom. Being able to live isolated and without community is not a sign of health but of pride. If God says we need other people, then it is humble and wise to embrace that need and seek to have it met.

The question is not *if* we need people, but *what* we need from them. We certainly need something from our friends, but it isn't what the world says we need. What we need are companions who will fight for our ultimate good: nearness to Christ.

So, then, how does that play out in friendship? What do we really need from one another? In my experience there are four distinct needs our friends meet that continue to bolster our love for Christ. We need:

1. Friends to deepen our joy in Christ.
2. Friends to battle with us.
3. Friends to carry us in our weakness.
4. Friends to be there for us.

With a list like this, it's worth saying that seeking friends who can handle these needs will naturally make us look for people who already know and treasure Jesus. Of course, we can and should have non-Christian friends, but it is good for those in our closest circles to share our love for Jesus. Proverbs 13:20 reminds of us that we should be discerning about who we let into our inner circle, saying, "Whoever walks with the wise becomes wise, but the companion of fools will suffer harm."

Friends to Deepen Our Joy in Christ

Take a moment and recall the most joyful moments in your life.

What memories came to mind? Maybe your wedding day? A perfect birthday celebration with friends? A family gathering on Christmas? I have no idea what memory you thought of, but I can almost guarantee it includes other people. Our deepest joys are shared joys.

God designed us for community, and one way we see proof of this is our pursuit of shared joy. When you discover a great movie, it's likely you'll find a friend to share it with: "You have to see this movie with me!" After discovering a great restaurant, the next thought is usually who you can take with you next time: "We have to go to that place this weekend. You won't believe how great the food is." The movie or restaurant is great by itself, but when you share the experience with a friend, the joy is multiplied.

The pinnacle of our joy as Christians is a shared joy. One day, because of all Jesus accomplished for us, we will stand in the very presence of God. We will see his glory with our own eyes and experience the goodness of who he is. But that isn't all. We will also turn to one another, saying, "Can you believe this?!" Not only will we experience our own joy, but we will be able look into the eyes of our fellow Jesus-followers and share in their joy too. There is no way to fathom how delightful this moment will be. Our deepest joys are shared joys.

This is one of the primary purposes of friendship: the sharing of joy. And God has given us so many amazing joys in this life to share! We need friends to share the joy of a great meal or a fun movie night. We need friends to laugh with and explore the world with. We need friends to read books with and create things with. Shared joy is great medicine for our hearts. And this is something available to us in friendship with those who follow Christ and those who do not.

But we also need friends to share our spiritual joys. Friends to tell about all the treasures of God's character we've found in his Word. Friends to worship next to and pray with. Friends with whom we can celebrate the faithfulness of God in our lives.

Our deepest joys are shared joys.

Our joy in Jesus always begins individually as we choose to deepen our relationship with him behind closed doors. But our joy in Jesus finds its fullest expression corporately, as we share the joy we have found in him with others. We are a saved people meant to experience the joy of knowing Jesus together.

Friends to Battle with Us

Choosing to follow Jesus means stepping into a war that's been raging since the beginning of time.

The Bible tells us that the world we live in is ruled by Satan, someone who has been determined to destroy humanity and defame God since Eden. He only speaks in lies and accuses God and all those who call on his name. Following Jesus puts us at war with him. Not only this, the culture around us is under Satan's authority and founded on anti-God principles. And to top it all off, the cancer of sin still lingers in our souls and our bodies.

That's a lot of opposition. Do you feel it in your life? I feel it in mine. And not one of us is strong enough, smart enough, or self-aware enough to fight this battle alone. When we fight alone we are defeated. Wars are never won by individuals; they are won by armies.

In the movie *Gladiator*, Russell Crowe plays Maximus, a Roman general sold into slavery after the emperor's wicked son attempts to murder him. He eventually becomes a gladiator and finds himself in the Colosseum with fellow slaves about to face their death. But his warfare experience has taught him one valuable fact: battles are never won individually.

Before the gates open to release their murderous enemies, he speaks to his fellow gladiators: "Whatever comes out of these gates, we've got a better chance of survival if we work together. We stay together, we survive."

Against all odds, these unskilled and untrained slaves defeat men with weapons and skills far superior to their own. Maximus's experience proved true: battles are won when fought together.

Christian, you are in a war zone. And this battle is not one you can see with your eyes. Can you feel it in the doubts that creep into your mind? In the accusations you feel in your heart? In the temptations that lure you in like a magnet? In the cultural patterns that come like waves threatening to erode all the love for God you've been working to cultivate?

This war is intense and sometimes debilitating. We cannot and should not do it alone. We need friends to link arms with in this spiritual battle. But practically speaking, what does this look like?

In my experience, it comes in the form of encouragement, speaking the truth, and confession.

Just last week I hit a wall while writing this book. My deadline to turn it in was approaching, and all my hours set aside to write didn't produce one word. Feeling defeated, Jimmy took the liberty to call up some friends of mine and ask them to pray over me. In a slightly weepy state, I arrived at my friend Brooke's house with another friend, Emily. We headed to the back porch where Brooke led us in a few hymns with her guitar.

As we began to sing, all the doubts in my weary heart burst to the surface: *Is God going to help me? Will he really be a good shepherd to me? Can he lead me through this?* Tears flooded my face as I forced myself to sing what I did not yet believe.

Worshipping together is front-line warfare. It's battling together at its finest. As I sang away my doubts in the company of friends I was freshly reminded of how much we need each other. That night we "addressed one another in psalms and hymns and spiritual songs, singing and making melody to the Lord with our hearts" (Eph. 5:19). After we sang together, my friends put their hands on my shoulders and prayed for me. This was the encouragement my soul desperately needed.

Hebrew 3:12–13 says, "Take care, brethren, that there not be in any one of you *an evil, unbelieving heart* that falls away from the living God. But *encourage one another* day after day, as long as it is still called 'Today,' so that none of you will be hardened by the deceitfulness of sin" (NASB).

The evil of unbelief is a ditch we are all capable of falling into. It was the ditch I was headed for that night. And the encouragement of friends shooed away my unbelief.

So what is biblical encouragement? It's *not* hollow platitudes telling someone how great they are. En*courage*ment is giving courage and strength to a weary heart by reminding them of what is true and calling them to whatever obedience lies ahead.

Encouragement from others keeps us believing, obeying, trusting, and hoping. When a friend confesses his doubt that God is truly good, we can respond by reminding him of God's goodness in the cross and of God's activity in his own past. When a friend feels tempted to believe that it's impossible for God to fully deliver her from a certain sin struggle, we can respond by pointing to the finished work of Jesus on the cross and all the evidence we see in her life that God is in the process of freeing her now.

We all need this ministry of encouragement and prayer from our friends, because alone our hearts grow cold and hard. Alone, our hearts give in to unbelief and slowly wander away from Jesus.

Battling together also means speaking the truth in love.

In a physical battle, you need someone to watch your back, to make sure no one is sneaking up on you, to check for places where your armor might have left you unprotected. We have the same need in spiritual battle, because sin deceives us. It darkens our understanding and makes us fools. So much so that it's possible to be walking in sin yet convinced that we are obeying God (much like the Pharisees).

Because we all have these blind spots, we need friends who can help us see. Friends who won't flatter us with half-truths but will speak with brutal honesty and tender compassion, telling us the truth about ourselves even when we don't want to hear it. Faithful are the wounds of a friend (Prov. 27:6).

This is a vital function of friendship that few people want. We'd much rather have friends who always tell us what we want to hear, who show us the false grace of excusing sin, and who give us a false hope that we can grow closer to God without repentance. But because sin is a poison to our souls and a thief of our joy in God, we cannot afford to forsake this part of friendship.

In fact, this is something I've come to trust and depend on. Alone, I am not smart enough or savvy enough to keep my heart from wandering. I need friends who love me enough to help me see those spiritual blind spots.

Yes, we need friends to help us see the sin we are unaware of. But we also need friends to be there for us when our sins are staring us in the face. Because part of battling together is confession.

The Bible is clear that our problems with sin won't go away in this life (1 John 1:8). It's not a matter of *if* we will sin but *when* we sin. And when we stumble into shameful things and grow attached to hidden sins, outing ourselves to other Christians is one of the antidotes we need.

Most of us are fine with confessing our sins to God, but saying them out loud to another human being is a different story. However, James 5:16 commands us to "confess your sins to one another and pray for one another, that you may be healed." Why is it so important to confess our sins to others? Because sharing our sins with others helps us feel the weight and severity of them. It's usually not until we share our dark secrets with friends that we find ourselves hit with the godly grief that leads to real repentance (2 Cor. 7:10).

Confessing our sins protects us in the battle against Satan's accusations. If we are the only ones aware of our sins, we have laid out the welcome mat for our enemy. What can we say to his accusation: "God doesn't love sinners like you. Look at what you've done. If others knew *this*, they wouldn't be so kind." If no other person is aware of this hidden sin, we have cut ourselves off from one of our greatest weapons: the truth-filled gospel message of a friend.

But when your sins are out in the open, confessed to a small handful of trustworthy Christians, Satan's accusations are easily thwarted.

Now you can reach out and receive the refreshing ministry of the gospel through the words of a friend as they remind you that your standing before God is not based on your works but on Christ's.

We need the fresh reminder that our sins do require atonement and sacrifice and that it has already been paid once and for all on the cross. There is no need for us to do penance, to make up for our sins to be right with God. We need to hear someone say that embracing the gift of righteousness through faith in Jesus makes us right with God.

The ministry of the gospel, the good news of Jesus, is most needed and most transformative when administered immediately after moral failure. And this is a ministry that we cannot give to ourselves.

The truth we need to hear in the aftermath of our sin is this: righteousness before God is ours by grace alone through faith alone in Christ alone. We need friends who know the specifics of our sin struggles, who can speak directly to our hearts that God can and does pardon our iniquity and removes our sins as far as the east is from the west.

> Alone, we wander away from God. But together, we stand firm in faith and hope and love.

We will not survive this war alone. We need friends. We need other people who are following Jesus to encourage us, to speak the truth to us, and to hear our confession of sin. Alone, we wander away from God. But together, we stand firm in faith and hope and love.

Friends to Carry Us in Weakness

Everyone will face seasons of weakness, where we are incapable of doing the tasks that lie ahead of us without help. Like the paralytic on the mat, sometimes we cannot physically do it alone. In those moments, friends become the extra hands and feet that we don't have. Friends may carry you by providing financial help after an unexpected job loss or providing meals after the birth of a child. They carry you by helping you move or jumping your car when the battery dies. Friends carry you by watching your children so you can go to the doctor or pushing your wheelchair after your surgery.

But these trying seasons are not always physical. At times they are emotional or spiritual. We may find ourselves in debilitating depression or with overwhelming anxiety. The grief of unexpected losses may have crushed all the hope that once lived in our hearts. Sometimes the weights we carry emotionally threaten to overwhelm us. Hopelessness may cloak us with darkness so thick that we cannot see through. Though the needs may not be as visible as physical ones, they are no less difficult.

In my own season of depression, a friend stopped by my house unannounced with a stack of notecards full of scripture for me to put all around me so that the words I would see when I look around my desk were the words of God instead of the hopeless thoughts swirling in my mind. Though it did not instantly bring me out of this trying season, it brought much-needed relief and hope.

When a grief is shared, it is not nearly as debilitating as when you carry it alone. Its sting is not so sharp. Its pain is not so hopeless. When we are grieving that life is not as it should be, we need friends who can enter into our grief and remind us that joy will be found on the other side in God's presence. That justice exists, and God does win in the end. And surprisingly, when griefs are shared, you'll find that a small seedling of joy and hope begins to bloom in that unlikely arid place.

As brothers and sisters in Christ, we have the responsibility of carrying one another to Jesus when one of us is unable. Sometimes it means just being present. Letting someone know you see them and see the hard things they are facing. It may mean writing a note to show you care and aren't going anywhere. It may mean regularly interceding for them in prayer. It may be paying for counseling if they are unable. Or opening up your home when they need to get away from their own space. It may mean remembering specific days that induce sorrow or hard memories. No matter how it looks, this is a ministry we will all need at some point. So until then, let's be willing to be this kind of friend for others.

Friends to Be There for Us

Lastly, we need friends who are committed to us, friends who are like family.

Now, you might be wondering, "Didn't she say in chapter 1 that our longings for stability ought to be met in Christ, not in one another? Haven't we established that we hold our friends with open hands?" Yes, I have said that. And I still agree with that. I cannot look at one of my friends and obligate him or her to be my BFF forever and ever. If they move away, I am called to support them in that transition by releasing them from owing me their presence. If a friend gets married, I have no right to obligate her to continue in our friendship in all the ways she did in singleness. God is changing her priorities and roles, and I am called to be a friend who gives, not one who takes. I need to love her through those transitions and be supportive of her obedience to Christ, not her obedience to my desires for our friendship.

So then how are friends to be like family to us? What kind of stability should friendship provide, and what kinds of obligations are right to expect? The commitment I'm advocating for here is corporate, not individual. And these corporate commitments happen in local churches.

There are two arenas where the Bible encourages us to be obligated to each other: the nuclear family and the church family. Husbands ought to cling to their wives; wives ought to cling to their husbands. They owe each other a level of commitment that is right and good. Similarly, church leaders are obligated to care for and be committed to their congregations, and congregations ought to be committed to one another and submissive to their leaders (Heb. 10:24–25; 13:17; 1 Peter 5:1–5). Our churches should operate as a spiritual family. For we are indeed brothers and sisters adopted by the same Heavenly Father. So it's right to be there for each other like the family that we are.

The Bible's answer to our longings for earthly commitment and stability is the church. Churches are local, committed communities of believers who are obligated to one another and who don't take their membership lightly. These are congregations who submit to the leadership of qualified elders and take seriously the command to regularly worship together and hear the Word of God taught. These groups of believers should take care of one another, provide for one another, and be there for one another. We don't need an individual person to be committed to us; we need a people.

But even within this church family, the obligations are never of an individual nature. Yes, my pastor is obligated to care for me, because I am a part of the church he shepherds. But if my pastor decides to exercise his care over me by asking someone else to meet with me, I have no right to demand that he personally see me. As two individuals we are not obligated to one another.

Of course, as individuals, we can choose to willingly obligate ourselves to someone for a season as our lives allow it. I can look at my friend who just miscarried and commit to stop by each day for a season. I can commit to check in and pray for that person in my small group who is in a season of depression. But ultimately, if these things are not volunteered, we have no right to make these demands of specific individuals. The commitment and stability we need from people will always be felt corporately.

Currently, our country is facing its largest population of single people in history. And the average age of marriage is now closer to thirty than twenty.[1] For all these single adults, they need a family. A community. A people to belong to. And the world would say, find a best friend. For those who follow Jesus, we need to offer a better solution. And it isn't individual friendship but a community of friendships.

But don't be misled. This is not an inferior option, as if marriage and family is the ideal and church family is the consolation prize. Quite the opposite. Our spiritual family is more real, more lasting, and more satisfying than the earthly family.

Jesus makes this apparent in one of his most radical moments.

> While [Jesus] was still speaking to the people, behold, his mother and his brothers stood outside, asking to speak to him. But he replied to the man who told him, "Who is my mother, and who are my brothers?" And stretching out his hand toward his disciples, he said, "Here are my mother and my brothers! For whoever does the will of my Father in heaven is my brother and sister and mother." (Matt. 12:46–50)

Jesus' own mother and brothers are at the door, likely trying to leverage their access to him as his blood family. But surprisingly, Jesus doesn't oblige them. He looks around at those with him, his disciples, and essentially says, "I have all the family I need right here."

What is Jesus saying? I think it's clear. There is a form of family that outlasts our biological family. A spiritual family tied not by blood but by belief in Jesus as our savior. Our friends who love and follow Jesus are truly our friends forever. They are our brothers and sisters in the faith, our spiritual family by way of adoption, as important to us as blood relatives. Our friendships within the local church are how we walk out this concept of spiritual family. And though we don't practice friendship in the same way we practice family, as we talked about in chapter 1, that doesn't make friendship less important.

In fact, it's our unity as Christians, not earthly families, that Jesus said will help the watching world believe God sent him. In John 17:20–21, Jesus prayed for our unity "so that the world may believe that you have sent me." Our union with Christ and with one another forces the world to deal with the reality that Jesus has come and is saving his people. It should force them to say, "If such a diverse group of Christians can do life together, flaws and all, and remain unified, then maybe this Jesus is who he said he is!" Church family, and the friendships we form within them, should be a high priority for Christians.

It's not just singles that depend on this stability from their church family. The church should be a refuge for all the family-less: the orphan, widow, and immigrant, the abused, the outcast, and the ill. For these, the church should be where they find a home, a family, and a group of people who will be there for them.

But sadly, that is often not the case. Because it feels safer and easier to huddle around our own family units and avoid the complications of caring for others, our churches often fail to provide the safety and security that many family-less people need. Changing this will take all of us doing our part to reach beyond our individual homes and welcome others in. It will take each member to make our communities welcoming and stable places for those who don't have an earthly family to depend on.

We have a lot of young singles in our church, and over the years many have found themselves in difficult financial positions. In these moments I get the privilege to remind them of the benefits of being a member of a church: "Remember, you have family here to take care of you. No one will let you be on the street without a home to come to. At the end of the day, if you cannot find a job and you do not have a place to stay, plenty of us have extra rooms in our houses for you to stay in. You're a part of this family, and we'll take care of you."

And sure enough, more times than I can count, our congregation has provided for those in need. Our friends Matt and Ashley have two young kids and once offered their home to another young family in a time of need, even though it made their space quite crowded. My friend Ruth is a thirty-something single who owns a home and has often freed up her guest room for single moms and college students, even though it inconveniences her as someone who works from home. Psalm 68:6 says, "God sets the lonely in families" (NIV), and the way he usually does this is through the local church. It's a beautiful testimony to the watching world about how good our God is.

In fact, just last week we had a college student share that she was behind in payments and the school had shut down her online access to classes. Not only that, she was physically sick and without money to buy medicine. She had already applied to several jobs with no word back, so her situation was pretty bleak. Since her parents were unable to help, she turned to her church. Within five minutes of voicing her need, several of us donated money to get her back online at school, she was given medicine, and a business owner at our church gave her a job. She needed someone to be there for her in her hour of need, and sure enough her church family was there.

Of course, if you have not chosen to become a member of a local church, then the benefits of this aspect of friendship will be hard to come by. I understand that jumping into a community of sinners who are in the process of sanctification is messy. Yes, you will be hurt in the process. But there is still no excuse, because we are commanded to gather together and submit ourselves to the leaders of a church. So don't wait for the perfect church to become a member because—spoiler alert—there is no perfect church.

> Psalm 68:6 says, "God sets the lonely in families" (NIV), and the way he usually does this is through the local church.

Taking Responsibility for Our Needs

We cannot do this life alone. There are legitimate things we need from people. We need people to share our joy in Jesus, we need people to battle with us in spiritual warfare, we need people to carry us when we are too weak, and we need a community that will be there for us like a family. There are legitimate needs we have in this life, but it is *our* responsibility to get those needs met.

We live in a country that celebrates independence and frowns upon asking for help. Success in America is defined as needing nothing from no one and being completely self-sufficient. So it's no wonder we seem to have an allergic reaction to asking for help. Most of us avoid it like the plague.

But sometimes we find ourselves in situations where the need for help is so apparent that it erodes all resistance instantly. The day I sliced my hand open with a sharp kitchen knife was one of those times.

At home with my eleven-month-old daughter, I made the mistake of cutting toward myself with a freshly sharpened knife. "I know what I'm doing," I told myself as I knowingly practiced poor cutting techniques. Well, two seconds later that knife had made a two-inch long incision into the top of my hand near my wrist. It was quickly apparent I needed stitches, and I therefore needed help.

We had just moved to Dallas, and Jimmy was out of town. I only knew a small handful of people. I quickly wrapped my hand tightly with a clean towel and began dialing the few numbers I knew. Most people didn't answer or were out of town. But Katie called me back and said she would watch my daughter with her kids while I went to the ER. That was great but didn't solve all of my problems. There was no way I could drive in my current condition, and I definitely couldn't lift my daughter into the car to get her to Katie's house.

The only other number I had was of someone I barely knew. Alissa and I had met briefly in the lobby at church the week before and had plans to get coffee later that day. I knew no one else, so I called her. After she answered I boldly made my request: "Hey, Alissa! I know we aren't supposed to get together for several more hours, but I cut my hand open and need someone to drive me to the ER. Any chance you could help?"

Thankfully she was free and showed up at my house twenty minutes later. She put my daughter in the car, drove to Katie's house, unloaded my daughter and brought her into the house, then drove me to the ER, sat with me for many hours in the waiting room, and sat next to me again while I got my hand sewn up. Then she brought me to Katie's, reloaded my daughter in the car, brought us both home, and helped us get settled. That's a tall order to ask of someone you just met. But what else could I do? I couldn't do it on my own, so I had no choice but to boldly ask for what I needed.

For many of us, we assume other people can read our minds and that they should voluntarily provide whatever we need. Many people leave churches for this reason: what they needed from the body of believers wasn't voluntarily given. But that's not how it works. When I cut my hand open, no one was alerted that I needed help. The responsibility was on me to get what I needed from other people.

Over the years, I've had a lot of practice asking for help. When Jimmy was on the road and I heard a strange sound outside, I asked a friend's husband to come check the perimeter of the house for me. When I was on bed rest, I shared my need and asked for help with dinners. When I was in a season of spiritual darkness, I asked people to come over and pray for me. When I moved to new cities and needed friends to share my joy in Jesus, I asked anyone and everyone I knew who seemed to love him, too, if they wanted to meet weekly to study the Word.

And you know what? In all those situations, I didn't always get a yes back. Sometimes I was faced with rejection. Sometimes people weren't available, and sometimes they said they could do it but never followed through. But if one person wasn't available I just moved on to the next person. Because the fact remained that I needed something from someone. So I prayed for the Lord to provide and kept asking until someone said yes.

God will always see to it that our legitimate need for other people will be met. But it isn't always in the way we would prefer. Sometimes the friend we hoped to do Bible study with just can't do it right now. Maybe the people in our small group are not the like-minded ones we'd hoped for. But the Lord is a good shepherd, and in his care we are never in want (Ps. 23:1). As you seek to get your legitimate needs met from those around you, thank God for what he provides, even if it isn't exactly what you preferred. As my friend Katie recently said, "We have to trust the Lord with what he has provided and be okay if we don't feel like kindred spirits. We have to be okay if we don't have 'all the feels' in our friendships." Sometimes it's the friendships we don't want that we need the most.

I need other people, and so do you. But sadly, because of our aversion to asking for what we need, to asking for help, many of us do not experience all the benefits of being in the community of faith. And that is no one's fault but our own. We need to learn to take responsibility for our own needs and seek out solutions to them. And at the same time, we can't take it personally if the first person we ask cannot be there for us. Because we know we don't need that one specific person in order to be okay.

The truth is, if all my closest friends moved away, I would grieve because of the preciousness of those relationships. But I would be okay. I need people, but not those specific people. I have the Lord as my stability, and I know that I can still get my needs met through other people in my church family.

If my friend Laci cannot be there for me, I can ask my friend Emily. And if she is unavailable, I can call Sarah. If Sarah doesn't answer, I can text my friend Abbey. And when she cannot respond, I can call my small group leader. And if that fails, I can reach out to my pastors and elders and let them know of my need and request their help to get it met. And if my pastors understand their role in shepherding the flock, they will pull their connections and resources to see to it that my need, if legitimate, is met through the local body that God has placed me in that I have been active and serving in.

So it is for all of us. We need to take responsibility for what we need from others. We need to boldly ask for it. And we need to give others the freedom to say no, understanding that it isn't a specific person we need but the grace God has for us in community with any person who loves him and follows him. The body of Christ is obligated to one another, and we should feel the freedom to act on those corporate obligations. Let's be bold to ask for what we legitimately need from the body of believers around us and also be ready and willing to meet these needs for others as well.

Faithful Are the Wounds

Redefining Our Enemy

Alissa had excused herself to the bathroom in the middle of our coffee date. When she sat back down, her disposition noticeably changed. I knew something uncomfortable was headed my way.

She gracefully navigated the awkward transition from "how was your weekend" talk to the ominous "can I share something that's been bothering me," and I immediately began racking my brain for what offense I may have unknowingly caused. I wore a calm face but internally braced myself for the wound I knew was coming.

Alissa very sweetly shared a few specific instances when she had just needed a friend to listen, and I had done anything but. You see,

I'm a verbal processor. At the time I was in the middle of studying and thinking through something I felt burdened to write about, so I was extra verbal-processy. Instead of listening to her problems, I had used what she shared as an occasion for a mini sermon.

Of course, I had meant nothing by it. Because I had not willfully sinned against her in my heart, my conscience had not been awakened to my oversight. But still, I had hurt my friend. So much so that she no longer looked forward to hanging out with me, which was how she knew she needed to address it. Because she valued our friendship, because she cared about me, she spoke up, even though it was highly uncomfortable for her. (I found out later that the reason she got up to go to the bathroom was to compose herself because she was so nervous.)

Proverbs 27:5–6 says, "Better is open rebuke than hidden love. Faithful are the wounds of a friend; profuse are the kisses of an enemy." I had a blind spot. A habit with negative side effects I couldn't see. And by God's abundant kindness, he gave me a friend who was bold enough to address it directly yet gentle enough to speak with kindness and compassion.

I'm so thankful for friends who wound.

What Did You Expect?

The story above isn't an anomaly. I could have told you about the time Kathy exposed my rudeness in using the pool at her house without caring enough to engage her in conversation. I could have told you about the time Erica shared that I had not been a cheerleader for her in a hard season but someone she felt she had to prove herself to. I could have told you about the time Kristy pointed out my laziness in being unwilling to call people back. Or the time Laci refused to listen to me detail the failings of someone else and kindly told me I needed to let it go because "love holds no record of wrongs."

You may be thinking, *This isn't what I signed up for! I thought friendship was supposed to be like a warm blanket, comfortable and safe.* And it will definitely be that at times! But we're talking about friendship with sinners. We're talking about walking arm-in-arm with human beings who still carry around the cancer of sin, who wake up with their defaults set to self-love. What did you expect? If we're serious about this friendship thing, if we want the real deal, not just the external shell, then this comes with the territory. Because the only potential friends out there are just like us: sinners.

Our problem is that many of us have unrealistic expectations of friendship. One likely reason for that is social media. Just as the false advertising of romantic comedies has likely ruined many marriages, the false advertising of Instagram—the place many post only the best moments of their lives—can ruin many friendships.

But more than that, we often expect friendship to be a resort for our flesh, an arena where anything goes. Your coworker sabotaged your efforts to get ahead at work, and, sure, as a Christian you should work toward forgiveness, but you're with your friends right now. These are the people who cut you some slack and give you a night off from the work of holiness. Let's have another drink and tell stories about how much of a jerk he is. But if friendship gives us a license to self-indulgence and bitter anger, then it is no friendship. It has become an enemy, luring us away from Jesus and into soul-threatening sin.

Don't be envious of the world's version of friendship, which doesn't confront sin but justifies it. Yes, this "non-judgmental" kind of community may seem appealing compared to a biblical community that calls you to holiness. But like the seductive song of the sirens in Greek mythology, it will lure you away to your death.

Acceptance Is Not Love

It's amazing to me how Paul's assessment of the world still describes our world today:

> They were filled with all manner of unrighteousness, evil, covetousness, malice. They are full of envy, murder, strife, deceit, and maliciousness. They are gossips, slanderers, haters of God, insolent, haughty, boastful, inventors of evil, disobedient to parents, foolish, faithless, heartless, ruthless. Though they know God's righteous decree that those who practice such things deserve to die, they not only do them but give approval to those who practice them. (Rom. 1:29–32)

These things should not be so for those of us who claim to follow Christ. It is never appropriate to approve of sin. Our friendships should never engage in gossip and slander and approve it as "sharing a prayer request." They should never justify envy and covetousness with "you're right, you deserve that more than him." They should never enable a friend's bitter hatred toward God for unexpected suffering by refusing to gently remind her that God has promised suffering to all who follow him.

> True love drags a friend away from the tracks when the train is careening forward, even when they kick and scream.

The "love" our world is selling is that of unconditional acceptance. A love that says, if you want to tie yourself to the train tracks, it's our job to cheer you on. It's a love as worthless as a doctor who never diagnoses or a teacher who never corrects.

True love fights for the greatest good of another. It tells you about cancer, though it brings tears, with the hope that you will get treatment and live. It tells you 2+2 is not 5, though it causes embarrassment, with the hope that you will be able to make sense of the world. True love drags a friend away from the tracks when the train is careening forward, even when they kick and scream.

Redefining Our Enemy

This true love calls for a redefining of what our real enemy is. Do you believe the Bible is the Word of God? Do you believe that what Jesus did in his life, death, and resurrection is good news? Then you must also believe that sin is the single greatest threat to mankind, the reason suffering exists, and the cause of physical and eternal death. And if we believe that, we must act accordingly, not ignoring it or approving it, but opposing it as the threat to human flourishing that it is.

Sin separates us from God; it disrupts our intimacy with him. Therefore, it is not a companion to be welcomed but an enemy to be fought. Thankfully, for the Christian, our sin has been paid for and its penalty removed by the blood of Christ. But that does not remove the present danger of sin in our lives. The ultimate punishment for sin is removed, but there is still a present power it wields.

If Christian friendship is united around a common longing for fellowship with God, then sin and temptation are enemies to be fought together. This is why the Bible abounds with commands to speak the truth in love to others, to address sin in one another's lives, and to restore one another to spiritual health by fleeing sin together.

Therefore, if a friendship ceases to take sin seriously, it has ceased to function as God intended it. Regularly making excuses for sin and avoiding moments of rebuke is a sign that intimacy in the friendship has become more important than intimacy with God.

Personally, this is the area of friendship I've struggled with the most. When faced with the decision to address a sin issue with a friend or avoid it to keep the peace, I used to choose avoidance almost every time. I convinced myself I was being loving, patient, or forgiving. But in reality, I was allowing my own sin and others' to go undealt with. I preferred fake friendships over real ones, so long as it kept me comfortable. But thankfully, Jesus is helping me be a faithful friend who's willing to wound, not a fake friend who multiplies kisses.

Putting Away Falsehood

For those of us whom Jesus has saved, we are now new creations and are called to a new way of life. We're told to put off our old self and put on the new self that is "created after the likeness of God in true righteousness and holiness" (Eph. 4:24).

One of the many implications of being a new creation is a call to truth speaking, since Jesus is the *truth*. As Ephesians 4:25 says, "Therefore, having put away falsehood, let each one of you speak the truth with his neighbor, for we are members one of another."

Truthfulness should mark a Christian's encounters with others. But it's not quite as easy as it sounds.

I moved into an apartment with my friend Brittany for my second year of college. What I assumed would be a fairly routine year turned out to be anything but. I strongly sensed God leading me down a few paths I had not originally intended to go. Paths that I knew had the potential to create some tension in our friendship.

As I corrected my course to what I was sure was God's will for my life, I timidly told Brittany where I was headed. But because I knew my decisions had caused some pain and confusion, and because I still had a debilitating fear of conflict, I instinctively backed away. Sure, we were still living together, but I was more distant and less honest about my life. In my mind, I was being loving. *I'm sure sharing about my life would be uncomfortable for her, so I'll just keep it to myself.* But in not sharing my life with her, I was actually cutting her out of it.

Eventually, because I was being less honest with her, I stopped feeling comfortable in our apartment. I felt that I had to walk on eggshells and no longer looked forward to coming home.

What I couldn't see then was that I was much to blame for this. When she tried to lean in and ask how I was, my answers were brief and surfacey. Truthful and honest friendship felt too risky to me with too much potential for conflict and hurt. So I embraced a safer route: falsehood.

When the tension grew to be too much for me, I came up with what I thought was a loving solution. I sat down with my roommate and let her know that I had found another living situation for the summer, house-sitting for a family, but would continue to pay my share of the rent until the lease was up. I told her I knew we weren't doing well living together and that this would serve us both better.

Not surprisingly, she was deeply hurt. She asked me why I hadn't been more honest and given us an opportunity to work things out. Truthfully, I hadn't even considered it. At the time, I thought it was loving to hide the truth from others when that truth had the potential to upset them. And so, in the spirit of "love," I chose to be a fake friend.

My "selfless" falsehood was actually a selfish love of my own comfort. I didn't want the anxiety that conflict caused me, so instead of fighting for our friendship, I chose to let it wither and die. When it came down to it, I simply wasn't willing to speak the truth to my friend and hurt her in the process.

Befriending others means being willing to be honest. It is far too common in the Christian community to back away from relationships without addressing the problems that happened. When we are hurt by someone, or when their blind spots make it difficult to maintain a friendship, it can seem very attractive to just back away from the friendship, to make up an excuse for why you cannot get together. But avoidance and passive-aggressive behavior is not love. It is a self-centered way to handle conflict in a friendship, preferring your own comfort above all.

Christian, you are called to something higher than this. You are called to set aside what feels easiest to you and pursue the well-being of others above yourself. This means being willing to lovingly speak the truth and to speak it right away.

The Immune System of Community

I cannot count the number of times friends have spoken difficult truths to me in love. Honestly, I don't think I want to know the version of myself that would exist without those faithful wounds. I don't think that version of Kelly would be very nice to be around. Each person who sailed into the tumultuous waters of conflict with me has rendered me an invaluable service. They were friends to me in the truest sense: sacrificing their own comfort with the risk of an unknown outcome, to help me grow into maturity.

> Speaking the truth in love is the immune system of Christian communities—a protection to the body of believers that arises when the sickness of sin threatens to impede upon our unity.

Not only have these wounds helped me grow, they have built confidence into my friendships because I know my friends are honest with me. I know they aren't just enduring me or flattering me. Now I know, if they have an issue with me, they'll tell me because they have in the past!

This part of community is one very few people want, but it is one of the greatest assets we have as believers! Speaking the truth in love is the immune system of Christian communities—a protection to the body of believers that arises when the sickness of sin threatens to impede upon our unity. It takes a high commitment to unity to be unwilling to sweep things under the rug. If we forsake this clear command in Scripture, we will be left with bitter and fractured churches that cease to effectively carry out the gospel to the communities they are planted in.

So how do we do this?

1. Decide When It's Necessary to Speak

We start by deciding when it's necessary to speak. If you're reading this right now and getting excited about all the things you want to point out in others, then this point is especially for you. Proverbs 19:11 says, "Good sense makes one slow to anger, and it is his glory to overlook an offense." There are plenty of times we may be offended, and it is right *not* to speak. It is a good thing to quietly forgive small offenses in our hearts and move on.

How can you tell if it is time to speak up? If it is a clear violation of God's law—like stealing, sexual immorality, or lying—it's worth addressing. Or if the issue puts your friend in danger, like staying in an abusive relationship or having suicidal thoughts—speak up. But apart from those two categories, it's good for us to be slow to speak and slow to be angry. Usually, the clearest sign for me that I should say something is when the issue causes me to consistently avoid my friend. At that point, it is causing disunity.

The next step is to *exercise restraint* by not going to anyone else. It is so tempting at this point to share your grievance with a third party and ask for advice. But Jesus tells us in Matthew 18:15, "If your brother sins against you, go and tell him his fault, between you and him alone." We honor our friends by going straight to them. So until we can arrange a time to talk with them, our lips stay shut.

2. Pull the Log Out of Our Own Eyes

There is one more thing we must do before approaching a friend about their sin; we need to pull the log out of our own eyes. Again, Jesus helps us with conflict in Matthew 7:3–5 saying,

Why do you see the speck that is in your brother's eye, but do not notice the log that is in your own eye? Or how can you say to your brother, "Let me take the speck out of your eye," when there is the log in your own eye? You hypocrite, first take the log out of your own eye, and then you will see clearly to take the speck out of your brother's eye.

The implication here is that we are also sinners. Whatever sin we have noticed in our friend lives in us too. We might not have acted on it, but we are also guilty. James 2:10 tells us that "whoever keeps the whole law but fails in one point has become guilty of all of it."

Before you approach a friend about their sin, take some time in prayer to ask God to expose any sin in your own heart, especially any sin that is of the same nature as what you need to address. Humbling ourselves before God makes us gentle surgeons when it comes to wounding others. We only wound when necessary, and we do so to cause the least amount of damage. When we have had to look at our own failures, we are more kind to others in theirs.

3. Set Up a Conversation

At this point, it's time to set up a conversation. (Yes, that means this message shouldn't be communicated via text or email.) If it's possible to arrange a time in person without distractions, that is always best. For me, that means finding a babysitter for my kids and sometimes asking my friend if she can do the same.

Within these uncomfortable conversations, I've found it's important to do five things. First, I cast vision for why I'm speaking up. I tell my friend it's because I love her and I love our friendship that I am sharing these difficult things. Second, I take responsibility for any of my own sins in the matter first and ask forgiveness for them. Third, I share my concern or my hurt. Fourth, I share the specific instances when this has happened. And lastly, I give space for her to process all that I said by asking her if she has any questions, any issues with me, or if she needs to think about what I shared and get back to me later.

I know these conversations aren't fun. I'm often wringing my hands under the table with nervousness and unsure of how what I say will be received. But I've seen the beautiful fruit that comes from dealing directly with sin and fighting for unity through conflict.

4. Get a Mediator If Necessary

The last step in this process is to get a mediator if necessary. Following his command to tell your brother his fault between you and him, Jesus says, "But if he does not listen, take one or two others along with you, that every charge may be established by the evidence of two or three witnesses" (Matt. 18:16).

There have been a couple of times that my first conversation with someone didn't resolve our problems. At that point, in the hope of preserving unity, we pursued a mediator. Sometimes this person was a mutual friend to hear us both out and help us see what we were missing. Sometimes this person was a biblical counselor. But in each case, having someone else in the mix helped bring us to a place of understanding, each of us owning our own sins and seeking forgiveness and reconciliation.

A friendship that is willing to sail into these tumultuous waters is a priceless gift. Let us put away falsehood and speak the truth with our friends, "for we are members of one another" (Eph. 4:25). Christians, let us "walk in a manner worthy of the calling to which we have been called, with all humility and gentleness, with patience, bearing with one another in love, eager to maintain the unity of the Spirit in the bond of peace" (Eph. 4:1–3).

10

Eternity in Our Eyes

Redefining Our Mission

In 2004, I stopped by the library to check my email (what a dated sentence *that* is) and found myself opening an invitation to join "the Facebook." I was a student at Texas A&M University, and a friend at Rice University had sent the invitation. At first, I wrote it off. I didn't want to get myself into some new online community that was just going to be one more thing to check.

But word spread quickly about this new site, so I, like thousands of my fellow students, created a profile and immediately saw why it was so engaging. I found many of my friends from high school already had profiles. Though I never would have been able to keep up with them in real life, now I could see what they were doing at college, who they were dating, and what their life was like. Friends I had just said goodbye to were suddenly back in my life through the computer screen in my dorm room.

I love people, so this new access to old friends was invigorating! I immediately set a path for myself to keep in touch with all those people I loved so dearly who were now only a few clicks away. I frequently made lists of friends I "needed" to check in with and send a message to.

But there was a problem. The creation of Facebook didn't give me more hours in my day or more emotional bandwidth for relationships. I was just squeezing old relationships back into my life amidst the new ones I was forming at college.

The result? I was immediately more stressed, more distracted, and more overwhelmed as the advent of social media began to massage in the lie that I had infinite relational bandwidth. I could have as many friends as Facebook would allow. Right?

The Limitless Lie

Modern technology attempts to erase our natural God-given limitations. Lights in our houses help us stay awake long after the sun has set. Smartphones help us work more hours, even after we've left the office. It used to be that moving away meant saying goodbye to people. Our physical location was a limitation. But with FaceTime, texting, and Instagram, you can stay just as connected as before. No need to say goodbye. It's just "see you on FaceTime."

It used to be common knowledge that we can't be friends with everyone we meet, but that's clearly not how our culture thinks anymore. Almost anyone we interact with, for however brief a time, can become our online friend. They are now a friend we follow and keep up with. Another birthday to remember, another Christmas card to send out, even though our physical time spent together was only a few hours. Our relational capacity is a limitation that our social technology is steadily eroding away.

Assuming we have no limits breeds a host of problems in our friendships. First, we become unwilling to let friendships come to a close. We have no category for seasonal friendships or assume that if we truly care about people, we'll always and forever keep up with them. But this is impossible! We cannot daily add new friends to the mix and maintain all the old. It's a recipe for burnout.

When we moved from Houston to Dallas, I was leaving behind some of the richest community I had known. The seven of us had weathered some harsh storms together and become very close as a result. But I knew if I hoped to have meaningful friendships in this new city, I needed to let go of the ones I was leaving behind. Keeping up with all my Houston friends would leave no space for new friendships to form.

Our command is *not* to love our Facebook friends as ourselves, to love our preferred friends as ourselves, or to love our oldest friends as ourselves, but to love our *neighbor* as ourself. And a neighbor is someone who is physically nearby. We must give preference to proximity, even when the digital world tells us location is an unnecessary limit. We need real flesh-and-blood friendships, not just over-the-phone-text-and-email friendships.

But there's another more serious problem that this relational expansion causes: pointless socializing. If keeping up with everyone is our goal, then we will spend every spare moment at coffee dates with friends and reunions of old groups. Socializing could be a full-time job. How many of us live in constant anxiety or stress to make sure every text is responded to and that we've caught up with every friend?

And to what end? Just to make sure we keep up with the hundreds of people we feel obligated to keep up with? Is this our purpose in life? To maintain all our many friendships?

No! Oh, please let us not live for something so small. As Christians, we are called to follow Jesus and live for him. To be faithful to advance his kingdom on earth. It's true that living for Jesus will mean loving people, many of whom we will call friends. But if our schedule is already booked solid trying to maintain every friendship we've ever had, will we even have eyes to see the lonely neighbor across the street? The widow sitting quietly in the row in front of us at church? The kids who need mentors at the local high school?

> We must give preference to proximity, even when the digital world tells us location is an unnecessary limit.

When I was a college student, Facebook became a distraction from the very purpose I was there for: to study and earn a degree. Technology may be doing the same to many of us today: distracting us from the very mission God has given us.

Remember Your Mission

So why are we here? Why have we been saved? What is our purpose in this life? Very simply, to know God and make him known!

We have already talked about our one great commandment: to love God with all our heart, soul, mind, and strength. But as we do this we are also called to tell of his goodness to others. In Matthew 28:19 Jesus told us, "Go therefore and make disciples of all nations, baptizing them in the name of the Father and of the Son and of the Holy Spirit." Paul echoes this in 2 Corinthians 5:20, telling us "we are ambassadors for Christ, God making his appeal through us. We implore you on behalf of Christ, be reconciled to God."

Friendship with God gives us a new mission. We are no longer to coast through this life, hoping it will be as easy as possible. We live to serve the one who saved us, as good soldiers of Jesus Christ. And a soldier doesn't "get entangled in civilian pursuits, since his aim is to please the one who enlisted him" (2 Tim. 2:4). There is a war going on, and the eternal souls of people are at stake. Keeping up with all our social circles is not the goal. It is a distraction.

How can we make sure our friendships don't distract us from the mission? Embrace you limits, have an eternal perspective, and reevaluate often.

Embrace Your Limits

"Do you not know? Have you not heard? The Lord is the everlasting God, the Creator of the whole earth. He never becomes faint or weary; there is no limit to his understanding" (Isa. 40:28).

God and God alone is everlasting, existing with no limits to his time, understanding, presence, and energy. When we attempt to live as if we have no limits, we are making the same mistake Adam and Eve made: we want to be like God. Resisting our limits is a form of pride.

Conversely, embracing our limits and living within them is a fruit of humility. It's a recognition that we are not like God, but rather are limited in our time, understanding, presence, and energy. Practically, this means saying no more often. Specifically, it can even mean saying no to *good* things.

Every yes we give is a no to something else. When we give a slice of pie to someone, we have one less piece to give to someone else later. So each of us will be required in our various seasons to exercise discernment about what we can and cannot do in regard to our friendships. Sometimes, to remain obedient to God, we have to say no to something good, like friendship with another person.

But isn't this why cliques form? Doesn't selfless friendship mean never saying no and always sacrificing your needs to be a friend to someone else? No. Selflessness begins with obedience to God, and that means that pleasing him, not people, is the goal. We should be willing to be friends with anyone, not showing preference based on what we get out of the relationship. And we should always be welcoming to others, choosing to extend kindness to whomever we meet. But if we hope to be good soldiers who don't get tangled in civilian affairs, we will definitely disappoint some people.

Though he was God, Jesus willingly submitted himself to our human limitations. That meant he disappointed people. In the very beginning of his ministry, Jesus healed many people, but he did not heal them all:

> And he healed many who were sick with various diseases, and cast out many demons. And he would not permit the demons to speak, because they knew him. And rising very early in the morning, while it was still dark, he departed and went out to a desolate place, and there he prayed. And Simon and those who were with him searched for him, and they found him and said to him, "Everyone is looking for you." And he said to them, "Let us go on to the next towns, that I may preach there also, for that is why I came out." (Mark 1:34–38)

Everyone was looking for him, and Jesus decided it was time to get up and leave. He had his eye set on the mission: "that I may preach there also, for that is why I came out." Likewise, when we keep our eyes fixed on the mission God has given us, it will be easier to discern when to say no and when to disappoint.

If we really are going to battle together, carry one another, and be there for one another like family, then we need something beyond shallow surface-level friendships. But the reality is, we cannot have these kinds of deep and meaningful relationships with very many people, because they take time and years to cultivate. As Proverbs 18:24 says, "a man of many companions may come to ruin, but there is a friend who sticks closer than a brother." These friendships that feel like family are built on trust and a mutual love for and loyalty to Jesus. That means we must be willing to have fewer friends. We must choose to have a few meaningful friendships instead of many shallow friendships.

Don't believe the Facebook lie. You cannot have hundreds of meaningful friendships. It's just not possible. So learn to let some go, and start being a good friend to those he has placed right in front of you in your home, in your church, in your small group, and in your neighborhood. Pray for him to turn those friendships into something that reflects him to the world.

Have an Eternal Perspective

Being a Christian means having a heart and mind set on eternal things. God has made us alive together with Christ and seated us with him in the heavenly places (Eph. 2:1–6). In light of this, we are commanded to seek the things above where Christ is seated at the right hand of God. We set our minds on eternity, not on things that are on the earth (Col. 3:1–2).

Our focus should be the eternal kingdom of God, because in some mysterious-yet-true way, we are already there, seated with Christ. This world is no longer our home. It is now a foreign land we are just passing through. Setting our eyes on eternal things works wonders for our friendships. It reminds us that what we long for in friendship is already ours: unending and unbroken relationships with friends.

My friend Stephanie from high school was such a kindred spirit. She loved Jesus and had a desire to see others come to love him. I loved spending time with her! But then we graduated and went our separate ways. So what could I do with all the longings I had to connect with her and continue our friendship? I could channel them toward their only true place of fulfillment: eternity.

The new heaven and new earth that Jesus promised to create holds with it the promise of eternal friendship with all those who call Jesus Lord. One day, when Stephanie and I are both there, we will have time to sit down together and catch up on all the years of life we missed out on and share all the ways that Jesus was faithful to us in our years on earth. I cannot wait for that day! This thought keeps my yearning for perfect fellowship with the saints aimed where it belongs: at my eternal home. And it frees me to be on mission now, concerned not with my social life but with God's kingdom and the role I have to play in it.

Of course, the thought of eternity may not bring comforting thoughts about all of our friendships. It can also produce deep sorrow and fear. Our friends who do not know Jesus will face an entirely different reality if they do not repent and turn to Jesus in faith. But this eternal perspective, though uncomfortable here, is actually helping us see more clearly how to be a good friend.

We can have truly meaningful friendships with those in our lives who don't follow Christ. While there will be limits to the depths of our friendship, that doesn't mean we can't enjoy their company. But in our friendships with non-Christians we cannot ignore the truth that apart from Christ they face eternal death.

A friend who doesn't follow Jesus faces a grave reality on the other side, and being a good friend means we cannot ignore this reality. That would be like ignoring the confirmation of cancer in someone's life, because it takes away from all the fun you want to have together. Or watching them drive their car over a cliff and being content to laugh with them on the phone the whole way there. Sure, you're having fun. Yes, telling them a cliff is coming will not be a pleasant moment. But what kind of friend are you if you don't speak up?

So how can we be a good friend to someone who doesn't know God? Being a good friend to an unbeliever does *not* mean preaching to them every moment you are together. But it does mean being willing to speak what is true and point them to Jesus as the only capable savior, the only solution for sin and evil, the only fountain of living water, the only hope for eternal life and unending joy. So be a good friend who models the kindness, humility, and sacrificial love of Jesus. And do so in hopes not just to gain a friend but to see that friend gain something indestructible: the treasure of knowing Jesus.

Reevaluate Often

As we dig into and invest in real friendship, the truth is, most of us will experience many different life transitions in our time on earth. We will move from children in our parents' homes to college students to full-time working singles. Some of us will get married and have children. Some of us will start ministries and organizations and churches. Some will experience unexpected health problems and terminal illnesses. Some will move to new cities or countries; some will stay. Some will experience many losses; some will experience many gains and responsibilities.

In each season, as staying on mission for God's kingdom changes, we will have different capacities for friendship. But in each season, we need good friendships. We must often reevaluate what it looks like to love God with all that we are and then love our neighbor as ourselves. We must fight for this in our own lives and encourage our friends to do the same, holding all with open hands, entrusting ourselves and them to a faithful Creator by whom and for whom we are saved.

Comrades for the Kingdom

As Christians, we can handle the ebb and flow of relationships, because the future is bright for friendship. One day, we'll find ourselves in a great multitude that no one can number, from every nation, tribe, people, and language, standing before the throne and before the Lamb, our friends by our sides, clothed in white robes, with palm branches in our hands, and crying out in a loud voice, "Salvation belongs to our God who sits on the throne, and to the Lamb!" (Rev 7:9–10).

One day, God will dwell with us, and we will be his people and he will be our God. And he will wipe away every tear from our eyes, and death shall be no more. And Jesus will say, "Behold, I am making all things new" (Rev. 21:1–5).

This world, as it is, is not our home. It is not all there is. We do not need to act like the culture, trying to soak up all the joy we can right now before it's gone. We have the promise of new life together with everyone who calls on the name of the Lord. The future of our friendship is secure; we can rest in that. So let's live for something bigger than the expansion of our own social empire. Let's live for God and his kingdom and "stamp eternity on our eyeballs."[1] Because, when our friendships find their purpose in something bigger than ourselves, they will shine with the rare brilliance God intended all along.

This rare brilliance is demonstrated in Stephen Ambrose's book *Band of Brothers,* in which he tells the powerful, true story of the men in Easy Company, 101st Airborne Division, US Army during World War II. Though they had come from many different backgrounds, their time in E Company bonded them together in ways few people experience.

> The result of these shared experiences was a closeness unknown to all outsiders. Comrades are closer than friends, closer than brothers. Their relationship is different from that of lovers. Their trust in, and knowledge of, each other is total. They got to know each other's life stories, what they did before they came into the Army, where and why they volunteered, what they liked to eat and drink, what their capabilities were. On a night march they would hear a cough and know who it was; on a night maneuver they would see someone sneaking through the woods and know who it was from his silhouette.[2]

Amrbose later shares, "They would literally insist on going hungry for one another, freezing for one another, dying for one another."[3] This devotion was so profound that many of the men voiced deep gratitude for the war itself, despite the hardships it created for them. Private Don Malarkey said it this way:

[T]his was the beginning of the most momentous experience of my life, as a member of E Company. There is not a day that has passed since that I do not thank Adolf Hitler for allowing me to be associated with the most talented and inspiring group of men that I have ever known.[4]

Comrades truly are closer than friends. We see this closeness in Jonathan and David, two warriors for God's kingdom, when David proclaims upon hearing of Jonathan's death, "I am distressed for you, my brother Jonathan; very pleasant have you been to me; your love to me was extraordinary, surpassing the love of women" (2 Sam.1:26). We see this closeness in Paul and Timothy, two self-proclaimed soldiers for God's kingdom, when Paul writes to Timothy in his final letter, "As I remember your tears, I long to see you, that I may be filled with joy" (2 Tim. 1:4).

> When our friendships find their purpose in something bigger than ourselves, they will shine with the rare brilliance God intended all along.

Comrades are closer than friends, because they unite for reasons beyond their own friendship. The men in Easy Company didn't band together to make new buddies, but for a purpose beyond their own happiness and success. They united to accomplish a singular goal: to win the war. And though most of us might not find ourselves in a physical war today, we are in a spiritual one that's every bit as real. But for us, the stakes are higher and the victory greater. The eternal souls of men and women are on the line. The glory of our infinitely good and gracious God is what's at stake. And the promise of eternal life with Jesus and all who call on his name awaits us. To link arms for this cause gives strength and meaning and joy to our friendships that the world will never know.

When we unite together, not for the worldly purpose of satisfying our own desires for friendship but with the eternal purpose of fighting side by side to see God's kingdom come on earth, we, too, will see the beauty and ultimate satisfaction of coming together as true comrades. With Christ at the center, our friendships will shine so brightly that all other versions will be but a flickering candle in the light of the sun. Let's stop indulging in the counterfeits of the world and instead live for our King and his kingdom. Together.

APPENDIX

Jonathan and David

Allies for God's Kingdom, Not
Covenanters Against Loneliness

Greater love has no one than this, that someone lay down his life for his friends.
—John 15:13

Few men have exhibited a better picture of this great love than Jonathan and David. In 1 Samuel 18:1 we see the start of their friendship. The CSB translates it this way: "When David had finished speaking with Saul, Jonathan was bound to David in close friendship, and loved him as much as he loved himself."

Wesley Hill, in his book *Spiritual Friendship*, grieves the failure of modern friendship to be the significant and satisfying relationship it should be for Christians. And I agree. We need deep, intimate, committed friendships with other believers in the context of local church communities. These kinds of close friendships are present throughout the Bible, Jonathan and David being the most famous. But while I agree with Hill's assessment of the problem—that our friendships today are often found lacking—I don't agree with his proposed solution: creating formal commitments between friends.

He hints at this solution in this series of questions:

Should we instead consider friendship more along the lines of how we think of marriage? Should we begin to imagine friendship as more stable, permanent, and binding than we often do? And if so, what needs to change about the way we approach it and seek to maintain it?[1]

Referring to Jonathan and David and the covenant they made with each other, Hill has this to say:

This sort of promise is so unusual in contemporary Western culture that we may be tempted to think of it as some sort of radical exception, as far removed from normal human life as the parting of the Red Sea or the virgin birth. In fact, however, such friendship was more like traveling by foot from city to city: an ubiquitous part of ancient and medieval life that we do not often remember.[2]

Using Jonathan and David as his biblical proof for the presence of such vowed friendships in ancient and medieval history, Hill encourages the expression of these formalized friendships today.

But while there are many things to emulate about the friendship of Jonathan and David, I would argue that their story is not an endorsement for this modern covenantal friendship movement. As you'll see, the covenant these two men made is different than the modern covenants proposed by Hill and others in three ways: its foundation, its function, and its fruit.

The Foundation for the Covenant

So what was at the heart of this famous friendship? What was the foundation? What drove Jonathan and David in their interactions toward one another?

In 1 Samuel 18:1 we see the start of their friendship when "the soul of Jonathan is knit to the soul of David" (NASB). What was the occasion for this knitting of souls? It was "when David had finished speaking." What is this in reference to? For that we need to look at the chapter prior for our context.

In 1 Samuel 17 we find David's defeat of Goliath. Here is the context in which Jonathan meets David. David has arrived at the battle, not as a warrior but as a sandwich delivery boy for his older brothers. Upon seeing Goliath taunt the Israelite armies, he offers to defeat the giant himself. And as we know, he succeeds.

The thing on display in this moment is David's loyal love for God ("How dare anyone defile his name?") and great faith in God ("He has helped me before. He will help me again."). We see it in David's words:

- For who is this uncircumcised Philistine, that he should defy the armies of the living God? (1 Sam. 17:26)
- Your servant has struck down both lions and bears, and this uncircumcised Philistine shall be like one of them, for he has defied the armies of the living God. (1 Sam. 17:36)
- "The LORD who delivered me from the paw of the lion and from the paw of the bear will deliver me from the hand of this Philistine." And Saul said to David, "Go, and the LORD be with you!" (1 Sam. 17:37)
- You come to me with a sword and with a spear and with a javelin, but I come to you in the name of the LORD of hosts, the God of the armies of Israel, whom you have defied. This day the LORD will deliver you into my hand, and I will strike you down and cut off your head. And I will give the dead bodies of the host of the Philistines this day to the birds of the air and to the wild beasts of the earth, that all the earth may know that there is a God in Israel, and that all this assembly may know that the LORD saves not with sword and spear. For the battle is the LORD's, and he will give you into our hand." (1 Sam. 17:45–47)

David cares deeply about God's glory and is personally offended that Goliath had defied the armies of the living God. He is utterly confident that God is able to make him victorious, even though he had no armor or weapons, only a few rocks. This is what is on display when Jonathan first sees him. And the end of this battle is where we see the two men meet:

> And as soon as David returned from the striking down of the Philistine, Abner took him, and brought him before Saul with the head of the Philistine in his hand. And Saul said to him, "Whose son are you, young man?" And David answered, "I am the son of your servant Jesse the Bethlehemite." As soon as he had finished speaking to Saul, the soul of Jonathan was knit to the soul of David, and Jonathan loved him as his own soul. And Saul took him that day and would not let him return to his father's house. Then Jonathan made a covenant with David, because he loved him as his own soul. And Jonathan stripped himself of the robe that was on him and gave it to David, and his armor, and even his sword and his bow and his belt. (1 Sam. 17:57–18:4)

What did Jonathan see in David that caused such a reaction? It was something he had likely only seen in himself until that point.

You see, like David, Jonathan also shares a unique burden for the Kingdom of God that stands above his peers. We see it just a few chapters earlier in 1 Samuel 14.

In the aftermath of his father's failure as king (see 1 Sam. 13) and his subsequent retreat from battle, Jonathan takes a big risk to do the one thing Saul was raised up as king to do: defeat the Philistines. Jonathan takes only his armor-bearer and moves toward the enemy.

In 1 Samuel 14:6 we are told, "Jonathan said to the young man who carried his armor, 'Come, let us go over to the garrison of these uncircumcised. It may be that the LORD will work for us, for nothing can hinder the LORD from saving by many or by few.'"

Jonathan precedes to run headlong into battle proclaiming, "Come up after me, for the LORD has given them into the hand of Israel" (1 Sam. 14:12). Jonathan's actions begin a domino effect that end up causing great confusion in the Philistine camp, giving courage to a scared and defeated Israel. And we are told, "the LORD saved Israel that day" (1 Sam. 14:23). All because of Jonathan's loyal love for and great faith in God.

We must remember that this type of dedication to God and his Kingdom is in short supply at this time in Israel's history. The people had rejected God as their king, longing to look more like the nations around them (1 Sam. 12:12, 17), and now the king God gave them has disobeyed God (1 Sam. 13:13–14). So it's no coincidence that when Jonathan sees in David the same rare faith he has himself that they are bonded together in unity.

And as we'll see, Jonathan and David stand together in immense solitude for the remainder of their days, supporting one another and fighting together for the same goal: to see God's Kingdom advanced and God's glory made known in their lifetime.

This, I submit (and I believe is substantiated by the text), is the ground, the foundation for their covenantal relationship. Contrast this to the foundation for modern covenantal friendship: eradicating loneliness.

Woodrow Kroll, on his website BacktotheBible.org, says, "It's a shame that we struggle with issues of loneliness while all along God's Word sets forth examples of committed friends like David and Jonathan."[3]

Wesley Hill also makes it clear that his case for "vowed friendship" is not birthed out of a desire to see God's glory reach the ends of the earth, but it is in response to the deep yearnings for companionship that are unfulfilled:

I think of the Christians I know—single and married, gay and straight, young and elderly—who are desperate for deeper friendship, and I remember the stories of their loneliness. I think of their disappointment in not being able to find as much intimate human communion in their churches as they'd hoped, and I wonder what can be done about it. . . . And that's why I'm inclined to say that, for all its potential problems, what we really need today is a return to . . . the possibility of vowed spiritual siblinghood.[4]

He later describes his longing for this kind of "institution of friendship" this way:

My primary question, over time, became a question about love. Where was I to find love? Where was I to give love? . . . I'm inspired . . . that there was an established historical ideal and practice—friendship or comradeship as a recognized, respected institution—that speaks, down through centuries long past, to [my] present need. There is, in fact, a place for love, and it's called friendship.[5]

But when we look at David and Jonathan's friendship, we see that they didn't form a friendship because of preexisting loneliness, nor because they were looking for a place for love. They committed to each other out of a love for God's kingdom, not their own desires.

The Function of the Covenant

As mentioned previously, the function of modern advocates of covenantal friendship is often eradicating loneliness. For singles—and especially those who foresee long-term singleness due to same-sex attraction—this kind of exclusive friendship is often seen as an alternative to marriage. But that is not at all the function of Jonathan and David's covenant.

To understand the function of Jonathan and David's covenant, we need to understand their political positions.

Remember, at the time of their friendship Jonathan is next in line to the throne. He is the prince, the son of Israel's first king. So when David is anointed by Samuel as the incumbent king (1 Sam. 16:12–13), it is at Jonathan's expense. Because of his father's failure, Jonathan will not take the throne; rather, it will go to David. If David had a potential enemy in anyone, it was Jonathan, the very man whose position he was taking.

This means when Jonathan initiates a covenant, it must have been a great comfort and assurance to David. Here in their covenant we see Jonathan surrendering his right to the throne, surrendering any authority he may have had to demand it himself.

This covenant very quickly becomes relevant as Saul begins to despise David and seeks to kill him. Think of the doubts that would arise in you if your friend's dad wanted to murder you. I can easily imagine a request for loyalty emerging from my lips: *swear to me you are on my side and will not betray me to your father.*

In fact, Jonathan's loyalty is soon put to the test as his father orders him to kill David (1 Sam. 19:1). But since Jonathan "delighted much in David," he warned David and then worked as a mediator between his father and his best friend.

It's not very long before Saul attempts to murder David again. With the help of his wife, David escapes the palace and flees for his life. Eventually, he runs to Jonathan and shares his burden with him, and it is in this moment we see the multifaceted purposes of their covenant. (It may benefit you to read the full account of this in 1 Samuel 20.)

David is afraid for his life and understandably afraid to return to his home, under the same roof as Saul. He confides in Jonathan and calls on their covenant to make sure Jonathan's intentions toward him are still good (v. 8). Jonathan not only reaffirms his dedication to David but also acknowledges his belief that David will one day be king and that God will eventually destroy all of David's enemies.

Of course, at this moment, Jonathan's own father is David's enemy. Not only that, there are huge implications for Jonathan if a new family line is taking over the throne. Dr. Thomas Constable explains: "It was common in the ancient Near East for kings who began a new dynasty to kill all the descendants of the former king to keep them from rising up and trying to reclaim the throne."[6]

So here we see their covenant is not only a personal protection for David but also for Jonathan. If God does indeed cut off all of David's enemies, then Jonathan and his family are standing directly in the line of fire. Jonathan therefore calls upon David to "show me the steadfast love of the LORD, that I may not die; and do not cut off your steadfast love from my house forever, when the LORD cuts off every one of the enemies of David from the face of the earth" (1 Sam. 20:14–15).

Jonathan and David were friends in a time of political upheaval when their families were sworn enemies. The fact that they covenanted together is not only understandable; I would say it was necessary in order for them to even be friends, because they had every reason to distrust one another. Their covenant enabled a friendship to exist. The occasion for any of us to need this type of covenantal commitment to establish a friendship is extremely rare.

Jonathan and David's covenant did not exist so they could enjoy undisturbed intimacy with one another, but rather so they could trust one another in a situation that fostered anything but trust. In fact, as we will see, their love for one another does the opposite of producing togetherness. It produces separation.

The Fruit of the Covenant

In 1 Samuel 20, after reaffirming their covenantal vows, David and Jonathan come up with a plan to discern if Saul is still planning to murder David. After executing this plan, "Jonathan knew that his father was determined to put David to death" (1 Sam. 20:33). At the appointed time, Jonathan communicates this sad discovery to David. They both know what this means: David must leave.

> And as soon as the boy had gone, David rose from beside the stone heap and fell on his face to the ground and bowed three times. And they kissed one another and wept with one another, David weeping the most. Then Jonathan said to David, "Go in peace, because we have sworn both of us in the name of the LORD, saying, 'The LORD shall be between me and you, and between my offspring and your offspring, forever.'" And he rose and departed, and Jonathan went into the city. (1 Sam. 20:41–42)

This moment is goodbye, not hello. Save for one moment when Jonathan sneaks away to encourage David in the Lord (1 Sam. 23:15–18), these two will never see each other again. The fruit of this covenant does not result in the fulfillment of their own longings for human connection and intimacy, as the modern understanding of covenantal friendship does. Rather, their partnership results in a parting of ways for something far greater than their own personal longings. Their commitment to one another is for the sake of God's Kingdom and the protection of God's anointed (David). And though I'm sure they longed to be together, their union in friendship is the occasion for their departure. And through tears and sorrow, they say goodbye to one another for good.

So we see that Jonathan and David's covenant is far different in its foundation, function, and fruit than the exclusive, intimacy-seeking friendship models being marketed today. But what then is the right application to this text? If making covenants with our friends is *not* the right conclusion, then what can we take away from their story?

How Do We Apply This?

First, we need to make sure we're clear on one thing: this story is not prescriptive. It does not prescribe that we all go make covenants with our friends. If this story were prescriptive, you could also conclude that, when entering battle, it is good to refuse armor and weapons and only bring stones. This story is *descriptive*; it describes the activity of two godly men in circumstances many of us will never face. But that doesn't mean we don't have things to apply to our lives.

Our first clear application is this: building friendships on a mutual loyalty to God and his kingdom is a great gift and asset to us.

Second, we must understand that, like Jonathan and David, a friendship built on a loyal love for God may cause us personal loss (as Jonathan lost his throne), separation from our friends as they follow God obediently (as Jonathan sent David away so he would be protected for his future service as king), and grief as they leave.

But their story also shows us just how fulfilling companionship founded on mutual love for God can be. Upon hearing that Saul and Jonathan had been killed in battle, David sings a song of lament proclaiming, "I am distressed for you, my brother Jonathan; very pleasant have you been to me; your love to me was extraordinary, surpassing the love of women" (2 Sam.1:26).

In a world where romantic love seems to be the end many are chasing, their story is a needed reminder that the sacrificial and loyal camaraderie found among those who proclaim that "all is loss compared to the surpassing worth of knowing Jesus" is far more precious than anything marriage can offer. Of course, we can and should hope to find this camaraderie in marriage, but marriage as an institution is never more precious than the unity of mind and heart we share with those who treasure Jesus.

For any Christian married to an unbeliever, this story should be an encouragement that it's okay to feel closer and more tightly knit with friends who share your faith than your own spouse. In some ways, those friends who also trust in Christ are your true family in ways your spouse is not—at least not yet—for all who are united by faith are united forever.

Lastly, this friendship reminds us that there is nothing unequivocally wrong with a close friendship between two friends. While I do argue in this book that the *pursuit* of exclusive friendship is not a sign of health, we must acknowledge that the *existence* of an exclusive friendship is not always bad. The difference is this: the pursuit of exclusive friendship is concerned with keeping others out. But this is not what we see in Jonathan and David. Though they exist in history as a pair of friends, I am sure that had they found another who shared their deep dedication to God's Kingdom, they would have gladly opened their circle of friendship. It was the scarcity of such sold-out God-chasers in Israel that limited the width of their circle.

So the point here is this: there is nothing wrong with a unique closeness between just two friends. Though exclusive friendship that actively works to keep others out is wrong, having just one friend who shares your love of Jesus is not wrong. Sometimes we are limited to one, whether we have just moved somewhere and have only met one friend or we are overseas in a foreign land with only one friend who shares our language. Sometimes our circumstances limit us, and we are right to gladly receive this gift from God. But, oh, how our joy increases to add a third to the mix who also shares our love for Christ!

In conclusion, Jonathan and David are a beautiful, shining example of Christian comradeship, of companionship for the glory of God. We are right to emulate them, but let us make sure that we rightly mimic them. They were not covenanting together to avoid loneliness; they were allies for the kingdom of God.

APPENDIX

Friendship Idolatry as a Catalyst for Same-Sex Desires

B ecause I have written a book addressing idolatry in friendship, I feel it would be a great oversight not to address the experience of sexual desires within idolatrous friendships. It is not only a common experience; it has a clear biblical explanation.

What I hope to do here is (1) establish that idolatry in friendship can awaken homosexual desires, (2) explain that we are all capable of this manifestation of sin, and (3) show how a biblical understanding of this issue provides both hope and liberty.

Wrong Worship Produces Wrong Desires

Romans 1 makes it clear that wrong objects of worship lead to wrong desires, specifically wrong sexual desires.

> For although they knew God, they did not honor him as God or give thanks to him, but they became futile in their thinking, and their foolish hearts were darkened. Claiming to be wise, they became fools, and *exchanged the glory of the immortal God for images resembling mortal man and birds and animals and creeping things.* Therefore God gave them up in the lusts of their hearts to impurity,

to the dishonoring of their bodies among themselves, because *they exchanged the truth about God for a lie and worshiped and served the creature rather than the Creator*, who is blessed forever! Amen. For this reason God gave them up to dishonorable passions. For their women exchanged natural relations for those that are contrary to nature; and the men likewise gave up natural relations with women and were consumed with passion for one another, men committing shameless acts with men and receiving in themselves the due penalty for their error. (Rom. 1:21–27)

In the passage above, the cause of this downward spiral is seen in the rejection of God and the embrace of created things. This, very simply, is called idolatry. When the worship of our hearts goes not to the Creator but to created things (like friends), it can birth a host of sinful longings that would otherwise not be present.

To be clear, some people have experienced romantic or sexual desires for people of the same sex for as long as they can remember. There was no event or occasion that initiated these temptations; they have just been a part of the landscape of life. Feeling tempted in this way is not necessarily proof of an idolatrous relationship. Sometimes our temptations do not have a specific external catalyst; rather, it may simply be the result of having a sinful nature and living in a world full of sinful people that is run by our enemy, Satan, "the prince of the power of the air" (Eph. 2:2).

For others, the experience of romantic or sexual desires for people of the same sex is awakened by idolatry. That is the variety of same-sex attraction I have addressed in this book, the kind which Romans 1 makes unmistakably clear is a result of idolatry. In the above passage the pattern goes like this: wrong objects of worship lead to wrong desires and eventually that can lead to sexual immorality of some fashion.

But this pattern is not only true in the idolatry of friendship;

it is true in any form of idolatry. The idolatry of money can produce a wrong (and natural) desire to gain wealth, and the desire for
money can drive one to sexually promiscuous behavior (as in the case
of Delilah in Judges 16). The idolatry of our bodies can produce a
wrong (and natural) desire to cease eating until the pounds come off
and can lead to compromise sexually if it gives us the affirmation of
beauty we so desperately long for.

So first, we need to acknowledge that friendship idolatry is sometimes the catalyst for same-sex desires and sexual immorality with
someone of the same gender. Let me be clear: it is not the *only* catalyst,
but it is *a* catalyst. Secondly, we need to own the implications of that
reality.

We Are All Capable

I don't know one person, including myself, who hasn't faced the
temptation to look to friends for things only God can give. It's a very
normal human experience. And if it's true that idolatry in friendship
can lead to same-sex desires, then, by implication, we are all capable of
same-sex attraction and same-sex behavior. And that is a truth many
do not want to accept.

The Bible is clear: we *all* have a disposition to sin. We are all born
going the wrong direction. Though not all of us have wandered away
from God down the path of homosexuality, we have all wandered
away from God. If our sin did not lead us down that path, it is not
because we aren't capable or that we are morally superior to those who
have. We are sinners just like everyone else, born dead in our trespasses and sins, worshipping wrong things and following wrong loves.
It matters little if those sins are culturally acceptable in the church
or not; each and every form of idolatry is a sin against the Creator.

Don't get me wrong; it is right for us to declare that any expression of sexuality outside of heterosexual marriage is wrong. It is right for us to hope to restore those who are caught in the homosexual variety of sexual sin. But to do this well, it's important to acknowledge that within our own sinful hearts is the capacity for the same. And sadly, this is where many Christians miss the mark: they assume that they could never experience or ever be tempted toward homosexual desires. But that line of thinking is not in line with the truth of God's word.

In Galatians 6 we find a warning attached to our command to call others out of sin:

> Brothers, if anyone is caught in any transgression, you who are spiritual should restore him in a spirit of gentleness. Keep watch on yourself, lest you too be tempted. Bear one another's burdens, and so fulfill the law of Christ. For if anyone thinks he is something, when he is nothing, he deceives himself. (vv. 1–3)

It is dangerous work to seek to restore people caught in sin without the awareness that you yourself are capable of the same sin.

If you have been spared this battle of constantly struggling with same-sex attraction, then thank God that you don't struggle with that particular temptation. But guard your heart from pride, as if you did something to accomplish this. Don't treat those who do struggle as less than; treat them as equals, people who, like you, deal with this cancer of sin. And keep watch on yourself knowing that you are also capable of the same.

The Truth Will Set You Free

I want to end on this important truth: the truth of God's word brings freedom. For someone who has sexual desires for a friend of the same gender, the world says, "You're just bisexual, and you didn't know it." But the Bible says, "You are a sinner in need of a savior." If the explanation for our temptations is that we are gay, straight, lesbian, or bisexual, what hope do we have for change? But if the explanation for our temptations is that we are sinners, we have all the hope in the world.

Christopher Yuan explains it this way: "And might God's word provide us a better framework for understanding the capacity to experience unchosen and persistent sexual and romantic desires toward the same sex? Yes it does. That framework is called sin."[1]

He continues,

In spite of a lack of evidence, the belief persists that people are born gay and that makes it okay. Yet, for Christians, innateness doesn't mean that something is permissible; being born a sinner doesn't make sin right. We must point people to a far more important claim: Regardless of what was true or not true when you were born, Jesus says that you must be born again.

It doesn't matter whether you think you were born an alcoholic; you must be born again. It doesn't matter whether you think you were born a liar; you must be born again. It doesn't matter whether you think you were born a porn addict; you must be born again. It doesn't matter whether you think you were born with any other sexual sin struggle; you must be born again.[2]

If you've found yourself tempted with homosexual desires in a friendship, whether that is a new sensation or one that's always been there, the problem is not your sexual identity; the problem is that you are a sinner. And if sin is our problem, a savior is our solution. And this is why Jesus came, "not to condemn the world but in order that the world might be saved through him. Whoever believes in him is not condemned" (John 3:17–18).

This is great news! It means that if our faith is in Christ, then our temptations do not define us. If our faith is in Christ, we are no longer identified by our past or present sins, or our past or present sinful desires, but we are now identified by our union with Christ. We are new creations, covered by his blood, adopted into his family, made into the perfect righteousness of God.

If your identity is wrapped up in your sexual desires, then every moment of temptation is a statement about who you are. That's a heavy weight to bear. Believing this cultural lie will color your entire experience in life and will prevent you from walking in the freedom that is yours in Christ.

But when we embrace the identity that the Bible gives us—that we are male and female sinners with a very great savior—we will find it's good news for our weary hearts. We don't need to figure out all of our sinfulness before we run to Jesus. We simply need to turn to him and ask him to do the work we cannot do: save us from sin.

Jesus is a great savior. Nothing is too big, too complicated, or too far gone for him. He can redeem it all and will turn it into something beautiful. Find your identity in Jesus, your great savior and the satisfier of your soul.

Additional Resources:

- *Holy Sexuality and the Gospel: Sex, Desire, and Relationships Shaped by God's Grand Story* by Christopher Yuan
- *The Secret Thoughts of an Unlikely Convert* by Rosaria Butterfield
- *Gay Girl, Good God* by Jackie Hill-Perry
- *What Does the Bible Really Teach about Homosexuality?* by Kevin DeYoung
- *Out of a Far Country: A Gay Son's Journey to God. A Broken Mother's Search for Hope* by Christopher Yuan and Angela Yuan

APPENDIX

Is It Time to End a Friendship?

In chapter 2, we looked at the Bible's clear position that Jesus demands our ultimate loyalty, to be our friend above all others. Our devotion to him should be so paramount that all other affections look like hate by comparison. Either Jesus is first in our life or he is not in our life.

So when a friend begins to lead us away from God and compromises our loyal love for God, it is a serious offense. Remember this passage we looked at in Deuteronomy?

> If your brother, the son of your mother, or your son or your daughter or the wife you embrace or *your friend who is as your own soul* entices you secretly, saying, "Let us go and serve other gods," which neither you nor your fathers have known, some of the gods of the peoples who are around you, whether near you or far off from you, from the one end of the earth to the other, you shall not yield to him or listen to him, nor shall your eye pity him, nor shall you spare him, nor shall you conceal him. But you shall kill him. Your hand shall be first against him to put him to death, and afterward the hand of all the people. (Deut. 13:6–11)

Again, we are no longer living under Old Testament law, so don't worry about the severity of the punishment prescribed. But what this passage does remind us about is that, regardless of how wonderful the people are in our lives, God is not okay when we divide our affections. Therefore, we must have a category for ending friendships—even with other Christians—for the sake of our undivided affection for God. It's better to lose a good thing than the greatest thing.

Jesus said, "If your right eye causes you to sin, tear it out and throw it away. For it is better that you lose one of your members than that your whole body be thrown into hell" (Matt. 5:29). An eye is a good gift from God that helps us see. But if that good gift causes us to sin, it's not worth having anymore. According to Jesus, being in right relationship with God is a far greater good than any gifts he gives. A friend is a good gift from God, but if that friendship consistently leads us into sin, it's not worth having anymore.

The question we then have to ask is this: When does a friendship hit this point? When is it time to break it off for the sake of our relationship with God?

The truth is, I can't tell you that. Each situation is so unique with so many different factors that only someone who knows you and your situation can help you discern this. For example, I've received emails from people in unhealthy friendships with cousins, with business partners, and with roommates. Each one of those situations has a different element (family, business, and housing) that must be taken into account.

Things to Consider

While I cannot give a hard-and-fast rule about this, I can provide some principles to consider in making this decision.

1. Remember you are an individual.

Deciding whether or not to end a friendship often feels like a decision to be made together, but this is an individual decision. You are an individual who answers to God for your choices. And it is to God, not your friend, that you owe ultimate loyalty and obedience. Instead of asking "what does obedience look like for us?" ask "what does obedience look like for me?"

This means you are only responsible for your walk with God, not your friend's. You do not need your friend's approval to make decisions related to your own relationship with God. Set your heart on the right goal—to reinstate Jesus as Lord of your life—and do whatever it takes to put him there.

2. Rightly define friendship.

In chapter 1 I said the best gift a friend can give is a commitment to fight for our joy in and communion with Christ. Conversely, the worst distortion of friendship arises when a friend encourages us, consciously or unconsciously, to place our affections elsewhere. If the latter is happening in your friendship, then it isn't really a friendship.

Friends fight for and desire the best good for one another—which is nearness to God. So it matters little if your friendship appears godly on the outside if it consistently leads you away from Jesus, not to him. It may be an enemy in disguise.

If that's the case, and if the purpose of separating from your friend would be to fight to see Jesus as your greatest good and the greatest good of your friend, then separation may be the truest expression of friendship you can give to one another.

True friends want more of Jesus, for themselves and for others. Be a true friend, even if it means you cannot be in their life.

3. Know that separation is a normal antidote for a stronghold.

If I discover that I'm addicted to Netflix, then I would fast from it. If alcohol had become a temptation I couldn't say no to, then I would cut it out of my life. When we feel enslaved to something, even if that thing is morally neutral, like Netflix or a glass of wine, separating from it is a normal antidote to help us run back to Jesus.

If a friendship has become a stronghold, a cyclical sin pattern, taking a break from it could be the best thing. That doesn't mean you will never speak to them again, which often isn't even possible. But it does mean ceasing from all the normal activity of a friendship: hanging out, talking on the phone, and texting. This gives you space to cultivate deeper intimacy with God and relocate your dependency on him, not on a friend. It also gives you space to pursue other friendships.

If you've become addicted to a friendship, all of this will inevitably feel like a season of wilderness and grieving. But that isn't a bad thing! God often tears down (which is not fun!) before he builds up. And though we are always eager for the building-up phase, the two processes cannot happen at the same time. Imagine if a construction company tore down an old building and started building the new one in its place on the same day. It would be chaotic and ineffective!

A season of separation is not the sign of a failed friendship. It may in fact be the beginning of true friendship as you both commit to chase Jesus as your greatest good. A season of separation doesn't mean you are no longer friends, but simply that you are friends from afar. God may one day allow you to be friends who do life together, but even if he does not, you have the hope of eternity. For all who share our faith in Jesus, we have the promise of eternity in the new heavens and new earth where we will enjoy one another's company in the presence of the One our hearts were made for.

4. Flee sexual immorality.

Sexual sins are a big deal to God, as is evidenced all throughout the Bible. Our command toward these temptations is to flee. First Corinthians 6:18 says it this way: "Flee from sexual immorality.

Every other sin a person commits is outside the body, but the sexually immoral person sins against his own body." If you are regularly engaging in sexual sin in a friendship, then the Bible has made your decision for you: run. Run away.

Too often these grievous sins get excused under the banner of "trying to save the friendship." Somehow, the perceived good in a friendship can convince people not to break off the friendship. The thinking goes something like, "So long as we clean up this little sexual sin problem, we can still remain friends." But this is not a biblical response to sexual temptation. The Bible is very clear: you need to run away. Flee sexually immoral friendships, and "pursue righteousness, faith, love, and peace, along with those who call on the Lord from a pure heart" (2 Tim. 2:22).

5. Don't make a big decision alone.

Proverbs 15:22 tells us, "Without counsel plans fail, but with many advisers they succeed." Before you make a big decision, make your situation known to a handful of godly men or women who can advise you. And don't make the mistake Solomon's son made, only listening to the counsel of the men he grew up with (1 Kings 12:6–16). Get the advice of godly men and women who are older than you.

Pull them aside at church on Sunday, send them an email, or make a phone call. You might want to talk through this appendix with them as you discern what is the wisest move as you seek to put Jesus in first place in your life.

Steps Toward Separation

If you conclude that you need to end a friendship, or at least change the way it is currently operating, here are some general steps you can take to do that:

1. Repent and confess.

Be honest with yourself. Though it is painful to stare our sin in the eye, we can never make it go away by ignoring it. If we refuse to face the reality of our sin, we will only enlarge the consequences and prolong the pain.

Be honest with God. Talk to him openly about your friend(s) and how you feel about them. Openly confess your desire to run to friends before him. Agree with God that finding your worth, purpose, belonging, and security in anything other than him is idolatry. Admit that you have forsaken him, the Fountain of Living Waters, and turned to a broken, leaky cistern that cannot hold water (Jer. 2:12–13). Ask God to save you from this stronghold of idolatry.

Then be honest with others. Find two to three trustworthy people (who are not the friends you're idolizing), and share honestly about where you are. Look for people who are stable, trustworthy, and mature believers in your local church. Tell them you've become too dependent on your friend(s) and have given more weight and importance to them than to God. Ask for prayer, accountability, and counsel.

Though it may be tempting, it is not wise to confess your idolatry to the friend you are idolizing. At least not at first. Though you will eventually need to talk openly about these things with your friend, to do so right away often backfires and causes deeper attachment. Remember, repentance is about you and God. It is an individual decision. Don't make it something you do with your friend(s).

2. Create space between you and your friend.

Sometimes circumstances don't allow for a complete break from a friend. But regardless of the situation, find a way to create distance. This may mean saying no to one-on-one times and spending more time in groups. It may mean refraining from intimate emotional and spiritual conversations like confessing sin and praying together.

If you live together, depending on the severity of the situation, you may need to discuss alternative living situations. This is where you will need the counsel of others to help you decide.

3. Prepare for grief.

Letting go of an idolatrous and dependent relationship is very painful. When you have put all your hope in one person, who is not God, it can feel terrifying to move away from them. Because you may have treated this friend like your significant other, this could feel like a break-up. Allow yourself to grieve for a season. Relocating our place of refuge from a friend to God takes time and can feel terrifying and does not usually happen overnight.

Talk to other trustworthy, mature Christians about what you are going through, and talk to God about it. Read the Psalms. Journal about how you feel. And know that this season of grieving will pass.

4. Cultivate other friendships.

This may be difficult at first if you have been used to the false security of having "one best friend who will always accept you." But remember, the only one who will never let us down is God himself. Cultivating other friendships helps us keep our hope in God, not in people. You will likely have to take steps to make friends when you don't feel like it. But walk in faith, and trust God with your whole heart, not a person.

5. See a biblical counselor.

While most people assume counseling is only for extremely traumatic situations, it is a great thing for everyone to do once in a while. If you have the means, consider finding a biblical counselor as you make the journey out of dependency on a friend and toward dependency on God. Having a safe place to discuss these things with a trained professional who loves Jesus is invaluable.

6. Get to know God!

Lastly and most importantly, daily cultivate intimacy with God. Chapter 6 of this book is meant to give you the tools to do this. If you aren't daily finding him to be the source of security, satisfaction, and approval, you will always look somewhere else. He is the only true, faithful, and reliable One. Nearness to God is the only motor strong enough to produce the selfless love we're called to have in our friendships. Nearness to God is the only thing that can free us to truly love others and not use them to meet our own needs.

APPENDIX

Healthy vs. Unhealthy Friendships

Healthy Friendships	Unhealthy Friendships
Fuel our desire for God	Reduce our desire for God
Make much of God	Make much of one another
Welcome others in	Foster exclusivity
Say, "God is your place of belonging"	Say, "I am your place of belonging"
Look first to Jesus in hard times	Reach out to friends before praying to God
Celebrate when others form new friendships	Feel threatened and jealous when others make new friends
Recognize there is no perfect friend except Jesus	Have lots of expectations and are rarely satisfied with friendship

Asks "how do we get more of Jesus in this friendship?"	Asks "how do we get more of each other in this friendship?"
Are openhanded with friends and okay with change in friendship	Feel like they own each other and are unwilling to let friendships change
Encourage obedience to God	Redefine or excuse our obedience to God
See sin as an enemy worth confronting	Justify or excuse sin in each other's lives
Celebrate and honor the institution of marriage, in their own life and others	Are afraid of friends getting married or growing closer to their spouse
Reserve romantic language for dating or marriage	Use romantic language
Act like individuals who answer to God	Act like a couple who answer to each other
Freely express care and affection through physical touch, but can function without it	Crave physical connection constantly and/or touch is a key part of the friendship
Recognize that Jesus is the only mediator needed for close relationship with God	Believe a specific friend(s) is needed to be close to God
Don't need to be the best in a group and celebrate others' successes	Constantly compare themselves to others

Healthy vs. Unhealthy Friendships

Are content with God's approval	Need a friend or group of friends' approval to be okay
Point needy friends to Jesus	Avoid needy people or act as the savior to other people
Know that they need more than just one friend in their life	Lose interest in other friendships when they find one BFF
Don't tie their well-being to a friend but to Christ	Feel despair, pain, or anxiety when a friend is inaccessible
Are not threatened by friends who are doing well	Only befriend people who they can help
Don't keep a record of wrongs or a record of their own good deeds	Keep tabs on others, always aware of who owes them
Are willing to sacrificially love others in hard seasons	Are unwilling to be a friend when they are doing more of the giving
Befriend those who are right in front of them, regardless of the benefits	Pick and choose friends based on how they benefit them personally
Are willing to be a humble learner in a friendship with those who are different	Avoid forming friendships with people who are different

Are willing to speak the truth in love to a friend and engage in conflict	Avoid hard conversations; prefer being fake to being honest
Are slow to anger and quick to forgive	Experience frequent and intense conflict in friendship
Don't wait for others to initiate, but willingly notice and greet others	Refuse or resist being the first to initiate conversation or friendship
Are not easily offended when they aren't invited to something	Are easily offended when they are left out of something
Know that they have blind spots and welcome the loving criticism of friends	Not willing to receive criticism or hard love from friends
Understand their need for stable community will be met through the local church and take church membership seriously	Cling to their individual friends for stability and aren't willing to be an active part of a local church
Are honest with their friends, even when the truth hurts and causes tension	Not always honest, especially when the truth could lead to conflict
Are willing to overlook small offenses and are slow to speak	Are quick to point out the faults in others
Know they cannot be friends with everyone and humbly accept their limitations	Are not willing to tell anyone "no"

Understand they can only manage deep and meaningful friendship with a handful of people	Try to make every friendship deep and meaningful
Know this world is not their home, and look forward to eternity for ultimate perfect fellowship	Act like this world is all there is and work to soak up as much joy as possible in friendship now
Rejoice to see others step in to help a friend	Feel threatened when other people help their friend
Have friendships based on something firmer than mutual disclosure	Feel the need to share every single detail of life to feel connected and close
Are more concerned with obedience to God than maintaining friendships	Hesitate to make plans that don't include a specific friend(s)

Acknowledgments

I give thanks to you, O Lord my God, with my whole heart, and I will glorify your name forever. For great is your steadfast love toward me; you have delivered my soul from the depths of Sheol.

—Psalm 86:12–13

There are not enough words to sufficiently convey the depth of gratitude I feel toward you, Jesus. You have delivered my soul from the hell I deserved and have freely given me the incomparable gift of friendship with you. How great is your steadfast love! Knowing you has been the deepest joy and most profound honor of my life. I cannot say it enough: thank you for choosing me! May my life and this book give you glory and honor and praise!

This book was incredibly difficult to write, and I frequently filled my journal pages with the confession, "I cannot write this book!" For years I felt God had assigned me an impossible task. So, as I marvel at its completion and consider what God used to make the impossible possible, the faces of many precious people come to mind.

Jimmy, this book would not exist without you. And you know it. You gave me courage when I wanted to quit, vision when I felt lost, and gifted me time as deadlines approached. Your sacrificial and servant-hearted leadership as my husband made this book a reality and kept my eyes on Jesus through it all. You have been my writing coach, my lead advisor, and my shoulder to cry on. You stayed up late, reading, editing, and rereading every word. Although you will likely never receive a thank-you from someone impacted by this book, I hope you know that the fruit it bears is as much due to your efforts as it is mine.

To my daughters, Lively and Sophie: your words of encouragement and consistent excitement about this book gave me strength to keep going. To my son, Benjamin: your joy, peace, and enthusiasm are precious gifts from God that have daily refreshed me. To my parents: Mom and Dad, you set me up for success early in life by teaching me how to be respectful, responsible, and trustworthy. Your belief in me and constant support is a greater gift than you know.

To my comrades in the faith, those friends who have linked arms with me in the trenches and who have fought side by side for the sake of the kingdom of God with me: thank you for showing me what true friendship is and treasuring Jesus above all else. To Lindsay Schott, Liz Parish, Laura Hobbs, Bethany Barnard, and Kellie Everett: each one of you willingly shouldered my burdens in this season of writing, spoke the truth in love, and prayed over me when I was too weak to do anything but cry. Jessica Adaway: I am much indebted to you for your generous help in organizing this content. You helped me put the puzzle together and find my way when I was lost. Ashley Samperi: our friendship is one of God's best gifts to me. Thank you for enduring with me over the years and helping me see my blind spots. I'm more like Jesus because of you. To Kelly, Caitlyn, Meghan, Kendra, Ashley, and Lindsay: our two years of doing life together, though brief, was one of the truest expressions of friendship I've ever been a part of. I will never forget it.

Ben and Donna Stuart: thank you for being a constant source of encouragement and wisdom for Jimmy and me from the beginning. Paul and Krystal Helbig: your influence in my life is more profound than you know. Your confidence in God's work in and through me has undergirded me with strength to move ahead.

To the elders at Stonegate Church: thank you for reading my manuscript, consistently praying for me, and often encouraging me in this task. It is a privilege to be under the leadership of such humble, godly men. And to my Stonegate church family: so many of you have prayed for me, supported me, and encouraged me in this season. It is a delight to do life with you.

Thank you Nancy DeMoss Wolgemuth and my friends at Revive Our Hearts for how you have supported my writing and this project! To Marshall Segal and our friends at Desiring God: you were so helpful in the initial steps we took to make this book a reality. Your help and support have been invaluable.

To Robert Wolgemuth, Austin Wilson, and the Wolgemuth & Associates team: thank you for believing in me and in this project. God has so richly blessed me through you all. To Jessica Wong and the team at Nelson Books: thank you for making this a more excellent and more helpful resource for those who read it. From our initial conversation, your genuine care for handling this topic well was evident and for that I am so grateful.

There are countless people who shared their stories with me over the years, many more who let me interview them, and more still who gave hours of their time to discuss these ideas with me. I'm grateful to each one of you for trusting me with very vulnerable moments in your life. Your courage and honesty have made this book a more relatable and life-giving resource to those who read it.

God truly has blessed me with great friendships throughout my life. From the years of childhood sleepovers, to the tumultuous preteen season, and the early adulthood of college life, I've had great friendships. To each and every friend in each and every season, Christian and non-Christian alike: thank you for making this book possible. By giving me the gift of your friendship, you've fueled my desire for everyone to have the ability to cultivate this irreplaceable blessing of friendship in their own lives. I thank God for you.

Notes

Chapter 1: Digging in Treasureless Fields

1. US Census Bureau, "Unmarried and Single Americans Week: Sept. 17–23, 2017," *Profile America Facts for Features*, August 16, 2017, https://www.census.gov/content/dam/Census/newsroom/facts-for -features/2017/cb17-ff16.pdf.

2. Megan Garber, "Galentine's Day: How a Beloved Fiction Became a Beloved Tradition," *The Atlantic*, February 13, 2017, https://www .theatlantic.com/entertainment/archive/2017/02 /each-day-is-galentines-day/516408/.

3. Rebecca Traister, "Girlfriends Are the New Husbands," *Salon*, October 4, 2004, https://www.salon.com/2004/10/04/girlfriends_2/.

4. Stefan Robinson, Adam White, and Eric Anderson, "Privileging the Bromance: A Critical Appraisal of Romantic and Bromantic Relationships," *Men and Masculinities*, October 12, 2017, http:// journals.sagepub.com/doi/abs/10.1177/1097184X17730386.

5. Robinson, White, and Anderson, "Privileging the Bromance."

6. Natalia Sarkisian and Naomi Gerstel, "Does Singlehood Isolate or Integrate? Examining the Link Between Marital Status and Ties to Kin, Friends, and Neighbors," *Journal of Social and Personal Relationships*, August 3, 2015, http://journals.sagepub.com/doi /abs/10.1177/0265407515597564.

7. Bella DePaulo, "Single People Aren't to Blame for the Loneliness Epidemic," *The Atlantic,* August 28, 2018, https://www.theatlantic .com/family/archive/2018/08/single-people-arent-to-blame-for-the -loneliness-epidemic/568786/.

8. Vivek Murthy, "Work and the Loneliness Epidemic," *Harvard Business Review* (September 2017), https://hbr.org/cover-story/2017/09/work -and-the-loneliness-epidemic.

9. Douglas Nemecek, "Cigna U.S. Loneliness Index," May 2018, https:// www.multivu.com/players/English/8294451-cigna-us-loneliness -survey/docs/IndexReport_1524069371598–173525450.pdf.

10. Shasta Nelson. *Frientimacy: How to Deepen Friendships for Lifelong Health and Happiness* (Berkeley, CA: Seal Press, 2016), xi, 32–33.

11. Wesley Hill, *Spiritual Friendship* (Grand Rapids, MI: Brazos Press, 2015), 6, 12–13.

12. Kayleen Schaefer, *Text Me When You Get Home: The Evolution and Triumph of Modern Female Friendship* (New York: Dutton, 2018), 13–15.

13. Donald Miller, *Scary Close: Dropping the Act and Finding True Intimacy* (Nashville: Nelson Books, 2014), xv–xvi, 65–67.

14. Scott Sauls, *Befriend: Create Belonging in an Age of Judgment, Isolation, and Fear* (Carol Stream, IL: Tyndale House, 2016), 6.

15. Vanessa Van Edwards, "Learn How to Make Friends as an Adult Using These 5 Steps," Science of People, https://www.scienceofpeople .com/how-to-make-friends/.

16. Paul Tripp, "Getting to the Heart of Your Words," 2008 DesiringGod, March 31, 2017, https://www.paultripp.com/articles /posts/getting-to-the-heart-of-your-words.

17. Resources: *Suffering and the Sovereignty of God* edited by John Piper and Justin Taylor; *Trusting God: Even When Life Hurts* by Jerry Bridges; *Be Still, My Soul: Embracing God's Purpose and Provision in Suffering* edited by Nancy Guthrie; *When God Weeps: Why Our Sufferings Matter to the Almighty* by Joni Eareckson Tada; *How Long, O Lord? Reflections on Suffering a nd Evil* by D. A. Carson.

Chapter 2: Marks of a Counterfeit: Replacing Jesus

1. Timothy Keller, *Counterfeit Gods: The Empty Promises of Money, Sex, and Power, and the Only Hope That Matters* (New York: Riverhead Books, 2009), xix.

2. John Piper, "Strengthen Each Other's Hands in God," Desiring God, September 14, 1986, https://www.desiringgod.org/messages /strengthen-each-others-hands-in-god.

Chapter 4: Marks of a Counterfeit: Mimicking Marriage

1. Rebecca Traister, *All the Single Ladies: Unmarried Women and the Rise of an Independent Nation* (New York: Simon and Schuster, 2016), 96, 98, 103.

2. Kayleen Schaefer, *Text Me When You Get Home: The Evolution and Triumph of Modern Female Friendship* (New York: Penguin Random House, 2018), 6, 44, 103, 123, 154, 167, 168.

3. Schaefer, *Text Me When You Get Home*, 154.

4. Albert Mohler, "The Briefing," *Albert Mohler*, August 31, 2018, https://albertmohler.com/2018/08/31/briefing-8–31–18/.

5. Robinson, White, and Anderson, "Privileging the Bromance."

6. Schaefer, *Text Me When You Get Home*, 217.

7. Traister, *All the Single Ladies*, 120.

8. Emma Richey, "Best Friends Isn't a Label, It's a Promise," Odyssey, May 30, 2016, https://www.theodysseyonline.com/best-friends-isnt -label-its-promise.

9. Whitney Joiner, "Are Girlfriends the New Husbands?" *Marie Claire*, January 16, 2013, https://www.marieclaire.com/culture/a7453 /girlfriends-new-husbands/.

10. Bella DePaulo, "Bromance Over Romance, Say Men in New Study," *Psychology Today*, October 17, 2017, https://www.psychologytoday .com/us/blog/living-single/201710/bromance-over-romance-say-men -in-new-study.

11. Cecelia Hopkins, "20 Christina Yang-Meredith Grey Quotes You and Your 'Person' Use Every Day," *Odyssey*, June 26, 2017, https://www .theodysseyonline.com/20-cristina-yang-meredith-grey-quotes-person.

12. Wesley Hill, "Why Can't Men Be Friends?," *Christianity Today*, September 16, 2014, https://www.christianitytoday.com/ct/2014/september/why-cant-men-be-friends-wesley-hill-friendship.html.
13. Hill, "Why Can't Men Be Friends?"
14. Wesley Hill, "The Pastoral Promise of 'Vowed' Friendships," *Spiritual Friendship*, July 24, 2015, https://spiritualfriendship.org/2015/07/24/the-pastoral-promise-of-vowed-friendships/.

Chapter 5: God Problems
1. Jessica Adaway, personal email to the author, August 17, 2018.

Chapter 6: The Saving Friendship
1. Jen Wilkin, *Women of the Word: How to Study the Bible with Both Our Hearts and Our Minds* (Wheaton, IL: Crossway, 2014), 31.

Chapter 7: Ripping Up Roofs
1. Rick Warren, *The Purpose Driven Life: What on Earth Am I Here For?* (Grand Rapids: Zondervan, 2002), 265.

Chapter 8: Not Good to Be Alone
1. US Census, "Unmarried and Single Americans Week."

Chapter 10: Eternity in Our Eyes
1. Jonathan Edwards, quoted in Adewale, "Stamp Eternity on My Eyeballs," Restore Citizenship, http://www.restorecitizenship.org/featured-articles/stamp-eternity-on-my-eyeballs.
2. Stephen E. Ambrose, *Band of Brothers: E Company, 506th Regiment, 101st Airborne from Normandy to Hitler's Eagle's Nest* (New York: Simon & Schuster, 2001), 21.
3. Ambrose, *Band of Brothers*, 21.
4. Ambrose, 22.

Appendix 1
1. Wesley Hill, *Spiritual Friendship* (Grand Rapids: Brazos Press, 2015), xv.

2. Ron Belgau, "Love, Covenant, and Friendship," Spiritual Friendship, September 15, 2015, https://spiritualfriendship.org/2015/09/15/love -covenant-and-friendship/.

3. Woodrow Kroll, "A Covenant Friendship," Back to the Bible, https:// www.backtothebible.org/devotions/a-covenant-friendship.

4. Hill, *Spiritual Friendship*, 40–41.

5. Hill, 20.

6. Dr. Thomas L. Constable, "Notes on 1 Samuel: 2019 Edition," Plano Bible Chapel, http://planobiblechapel.org/tcon/notes/pdf/1samuel.pdf.

Appendix 2

1. Christopher Yuan, "Is Anyone Born Gay?," Desiring God, September 8, 2018, https://www.desiringgod.org/articles/is-anyone-born-gay.

2. Yuan, "Is Anyone Born Gay?"

About the Author

Kelly Needham is married to singer/songwriter and speaker Jimmy Needham. She first began writing and speaking to his fan base in 2008 as they traveled together and has since garnered a much wider platform. Kelly is a regular contributor for *Revive Our Hearts*, and her writing has been featured at Desiring God, The Gospel Coalition, The Ethics and Religious Liberties Commission, Eternal Perspectives Ministries, and Crosswalk. She has been on staff at two different churches, serving in youth, college, and women's ministry. Whether writing or speaking, Kelly's aim is to convince as many people as possible that nothing compares to knowing Jesus. She and Jimmy live in the Dallas area with their three children, Lively, Sophia, and Benjamin. You can find more of her writing and speaking at kellyneedham.com or follow her on social media:

Instagram: @kellyneedham
Twitter: @kellyneedham
Facebook: @mrskellyneedham